Stem Cell Governance and Ethics

This book explores the ethical and governance concerns of stem cell technology, taking a comparative approach between countries of differing socio-economic status.

The book provides a typology of different stem cell types and discusses key ethical issues surrounding the use of human stem cells in research. Topics covered include the moral status of human embryos, various religious perspectives, and the challenges posed by unproven stem cell interventions. The book also examines the existing governance frameworks in the United Kingdom, Singapore, and Malaysia, identifying the laws, guidelines, and advisory bodies established to address the identified ethical issues. Applicable lessons on establishing robust regulatory frameworks, fostering public trust, and ensuring responsible research practices are outlined.

By providing a comparative analysis of the interplay between ethics, governance, and the socio-economic contexts of these three commonwealth countries, this book will interest health law, research ethics, and bioethics scholars.

Mohammad Firdaus Bin Abdul Aziz is Senior Lecturer and Deputy Dean of Research and Innovation at the Faculty of Law, Universiti Malaya. He obtained his DPhil from the University of Oxford. Currently, he is a co-investigator on a UK Wellcome Trust-funded initiative aimed at establishing a bioethics network in Southeast Asia and a co-investigator on the US NIH Fogarty grant, which focuses on developing a master's program in health research ethics at Universiti Malaya.

Routledge Studies in Asian Law

Constitutional Remedies in Asia
Edited by Po Jen Yap

Chinese Legal Culture and Constitutional Order
Shiping Hua

Land Law and Disputes in Asia
In Search of an Alternative for Development
Edited by Brian Z. Tamanaha, Narufumi Kadomatsu and Yuka Kaneko

China's Foreign Investment Legal Regime
Progress and Limitations
Yuwen Li and Cheng Bian

Philosophy of Law in Korea
Acceptance, Engagement and Social Change
Jeong-Oh Kim, Hak-Tai Kim, Joon-Seok Park, Dong-Ryong Shin

The Law and Regulation of Public Health
Global Perspectives on Hong Kong
Eric C. Ip

State Administrative Law in Indonesia
M. Zaenul Muttaqin

Stem Cell Governance and Ethics
Mohammad Firdaus Bin Abdul Aziz

For more information about this series, please visit: https://www.routledge.com/asianstudies/series/RSIAL

Stem Cell Governance and Ethics

Mohammad Firdaus Bin Abdul Aziz

Routledge
Taylor & Francis Group
LONDON AND NEW YORK

First published 2025
by Routledge
4 Park Square, Milton Park, Abingdon, Oxon, OX14 4RN

and by Routledge
605 Third Avenue, New York, NY 10158

Routledge is an imprint of the Taylor & Francis Group, an informa business

British Library Cataloguing-in-Publication Data
A catalogue record for this book is available from the British Library

Library of Congress Cataloging-in-Publication Data
Names: Aziz, Mohammad Firdaus Bin Abdul, author.
Title: Stem cell governance and ethics / Mohammad Firdaus Bin Abdul Aziz.
Description: Abingdon, Oxon [UK] ; New York, NY : Routledge, 2025. | Series: Routledge studies in Asian law | Includes bibliographical references and index.
Identifiers: LCCN 2024054171 (print) | LCCN 2024054172 (ebook) | ISBN 9781032951669 (hardback) | ISBN 9781032951676 (paperback) | ISBN 9781003583479 (ebook)
Subjects: LCSH: Stem cells—Research—Law and legislation. | Stem cells—Moral and ethical aspects. | Genetic engineering—Law and legislation.
Classification: LCC K3611.G46 A95 2025 (print) | LCC K3611.G46 (ebook) | DDC 174.2/8—dc23/eng/20241118
LC record available at https://lccn.loc.gov/2024054171
LC ebook record available at https://lccn.loc.gov/2024054172

ISBN: 9781032951669 (hbk)
ISBN: 9781032951676 (pbk)
ISBN: 9781003583479 (ebk)

DOI: 10.4324/9781003583479

Typeset in Times New Roman
by Apex CoVantage, LLC

Contents

1 Overview

1.1 Introduction

Human stem cells, in particular the embryonic stem cells are the precursor cells in the human body that have unique characteristics and remarkable ability to give rise to new tissues and potentially organs. This notable and exceptional ability is very promising and particularly useful to research possible treatments that could heal or replace damaged tissues and organs. Aware of this promising research, many countries are striving to utilise human embryonic stem cells which could lead to the realisation of stem cell therapies for many diseases and degenerations due to its pluripotency.

The United Kingdom, Singapore, and Malaysia are just three of the many countries across the globe that are encouraging progress in this field to ensure their positions at the forefront of human stem cell research (hSCR). However, this research has brought about ethical controversy particularly involving the use of human embryos because it requires scientists to destroy the embryos, which is perceived by many as the first stage of the beginnings of human life. The public at large, religious scholars, policymakers, and many more have divided in their approach towards allowing and regulating this area. This book will unravel the complexities of stem cell technology and its profound impact on the medical and regulatory landscape. The exploration will be carried out based on two main themes namely (i) the ethical conundrums posed by the technology, particularly the ethical issues surrounding the use of human embryos for research purposes and (ii) the governance issues and challenges in addressing the ethical issues faced by developing nations with lower socioeconomic status such as Malaysia compared to the regulatory responses taken by higher income nations such as the United Kingdom and Singapore.

The interest behind this book project is developed from a concern grounded in reading that demonstrates human embryonic stem cell (hESC) research is highly contentious. Therefore, the regulatory system for hSCR particularly hESC research is crucial and critically needed to provide clarity and ensure ethical conduct. For instance, Isasi and Knoppers (2006) argue

DOI: 10.4324/9781003583479-1

that ethical compliance measures such as ethical justifications for the use of human embryos, ethics review, and centralised and independent authority empowered to grant licences and monitor the conduct of research, are vital and they should be incorporated in a regulatory framework. This framework is not merely for ensuring compliance but studies have shown that it is equivalently important for researchers to work in an environment with a clear ethical guidance, which would help their research progress (Caulfield et al., 2012). In addition, the establishment of the International Society of Stem Cell Research Society (ISSCR) indicates the international effort to uphold such values. The ISSCR has produced guidelines that provide "a set of recommendations for researchers, clinicians, and oversight groups to aid their decision-making", which aspires to facilitate the advancement of this area, particularly to translate stem cell science to the clinic ethically and safely (Scadden & Srivastava, 2012).

The measures discussed by Isasi and Knoppers (2006) appear to be absent in Malaysia's current framework. Without these measures in the current regulatory framework, this suggests it is inadequate and not on par with other countries that have a more established system. Given there are jurisdictions, especially the United K which have established a thorough regulatory system to regulate this challenging area, Malaysia could potentially learn and benefit from them.

In so doing, this book sets out three objectives; (i) to offer an overview of the significance and impact of utilising human stem cells in the realm of healthcare research, aiming to shed light on the potential of these biological building blocks in revolutionising the medical sector; (ii) to delve into the heart of the matter by dissecting the moral and bioethical concerns that have sparked off the contentious discourse surrounding the use of human embryos for stem cell research. In particular, the focus will be on the central issue of the moral status of human embryos, which has ignited a controversial debate among both proponents and detractors; and (iii) to illuminate the governance responses taken by the under-studied jurisdictions in addressing the ethical issues associated with the use of human embryos for research purposes stem cells, positing a global perspective that considers the diverse socioeconomic, cultural, and religious landscapes of different countries, particularly between developing and developed nations.

This book does not intend to produce a definitive list of recommendations as to how Malaysia should regulate hSCR activities, especially the use of human embryos for research purposes, but rather to point out the inadequacy of regulatory responses by Malaysia compared to the approaches adopted by the selected jurisdictions and the regulatory measures that can be considered by Malaysian policymakers to further improve the existing regulatory framework for hSCR. The United Kingdom and Singapore have been selected because Malaysia shares similar legal foundations with these two nations, both of which are part of the Commonwealth.

1.2 Structure of the book

This book seeks to explore the multifaceted nature of stem cells, addressing not only their scientific potential but also the ethical complexities that arise from their use. The aim is to provide a comprehensive overview that informs, challenges, and engages readers—from laypersons to professionals—in the discourse surrounding stem cell research. To facilitate understanding, the book is structured into five distinct chapters.

Chapter 1: Overview

This chapter outlines the book's objectives and structure, setting the stage for an in-depth exploration of stem cells, their applications, ethical implications, and regulatory frameworks. Additionally, this chapter delves into why scientists consider stem cells crucial for revolutionising the treatment landscape, offering hope for cures where none currently exist. By the end of this chapter, readers will understand the importance of human stem cell research in developing stem cell-based therapies, particularly in relation to medical conditions which are currently incurable by conventional medicine.

Chapter 2: The controversial issues of human embryos

This chapter explores the ethical dilemmas surrounding human stem cell research, with a particular focus on the controversial use of human embryos. The complexities of moral status, informed by various religious perspectives, are examined to provide a nuanced understanding of the debate. The discussion largely focuses on the implications of the 14-day rule and briefly touches on related issues surrounding egg donation and unproven stem cell interventions.

Chapter 3: The governance framework in the United Kingdom, Singapore, and Malaysia

Here, the book shifts to a discussion of existing international regulations governing stem cell research. By comparing the governance frameworks of three selected jurisdictions—namely the United Kingdom, Singapore, and Malaysia—this chapter examines how these countries address the ethical issues previously discussed. This chapter aims to shed light on the established laws, guidelines, and advisory bodies that play pivotal roles in regulating this evolving field.

Chapter 4: Regulatory response to ethical issues

Building on the preceding chapter's examination, Chapter 4 discusses the diverse approaches taken by the United Kingdom, Singapore, and Malaysia in response to ethical challenges. It critically evaluates how Malaysia can harmonise secular bioethics with religious values in navigating issues related to the use of human embryos and eggs. The chapter also emphasises the need for Malaysia to find a balance to develop a more robust governance framework and at the same time recognise its limitations as a developing nation regarding its resource allocation in the development of stem cell technologies.

Chapter 5: The way forward for Malaysia

This concluding chapter summarises the critical insights gained throughout the book, focusing on governance aspects particularly relevant to Malaysia. It advocates for revisiting the bioethical debates concerning human embryos and the significance of the 14-day rule within the local context. The chapter also proposes legislative measures aimed at enhancing protection for human embryos and ensuring responsible governance of stem cell research in Malaysia.

1.3 Introduction to stem cells

Stem cells are often referred to as the "body's natural reservoir", representing the most fundamental cellular components from which all other cells, tissues and organs are derived (EuroStemCell). These remarkable cells are characterised by their unique abilities: they can self-renew, creating copies of themselves, and they possess the capacity to differentiate into a wide variety of specialised cells, forming tissues and organs essential for bodily function.

1.3.1 The potency landscape of stem cells: totipotency, pluripotency, and multipotency

The differentiation potential of stem cells varies based on their potency, which can be categorised into three primary types: totipotency, pluripotency, and multipotency (Campbell & Reece, 2005). Essentially, the potency of the stem cells decreases as they become more mature, however, they still have the capability to self-renew.

Totipotent stem cells

Totipotent stem cells hold the remarkable ability to differentiate into any cell type, including both embryonic and placental tissues. This means that a totipotent cell can give rise to an entirely new organism. During the early stages of development, such as the first few rounds of cell division post-fertilisation, embryonic stem cells (ESCs) remain totipotent. This characteristic is crucial for the initial stages of human development, allowing for the formation of all cell types necessary to create a fully functional organism.

Pluripotent stem cells

As development progresses, the potency of stem cells transitions from totipotency to pluripotency. Pluripotent stem cells can differentiate into nearly all cell types found in the human body, except for those involved in forming the placenta (trophoblast cells). Embryonic stem cells fall into this category, making them vital for research due to their extensive differentiation potential. Their ability to generate virtually any cell type has led researchers to regard them as essential for developing therapies for a range of degenerative diseases.

Multipotent stem cells

In contrast, multipotent stem cells are usually associated with adult tissues. These cells have a more restricted differentiation capacity, typically producing only the specialised cells related to their specific tissue. Despite this limitation, multipotent stem cells still retain their ability to self-renew, albeit at a reduced potency compared to their pluripotent counterparts. For instance, hematopoietic stem cells (HSCs) found in bone marrow can give rise to various blood cells but cannot transform into cells of other lineages, such as nerve or muscle cells.

The implications of these unique properties are profound, leading researchers to advocate for the use of stem cells in scientific research with the potential to bring considerable benefits to humankind. This potential encompasses various stem cell types beyond embryonic and adult stem cells; it includes mesenchymal stem cells (MSCs), cancer stem cells (CSCs) (Arney, 2008; Barker et al., 2009) hematopoietic (blood) stem cells (HSCs) (Daley & Scadden, 2008), spermatogonial stem cells (SSCs) (Firlej et al., 2012) induced pluripotent stem cells (iPSCs), foetal stem cells, and many more. Among these, human embryonic stem cells are often regarded as the "gold standard" in human stem cell research (hSCR) due to their superior pluripotency and ability to generate diverse cell types (Crook et al., 2007; Gawrylewski, 2008; Heng et al., 2009).

1.3.2 Techniques for deriving human stem cells

The field of stem cell research has witnessed considerable advancements in the development of techniques to derive human stem cells. These methods have broadened the horizons for generating stem cells for therapeutic purposes. Some prominent techniques are highlighted in the following.

In vitro fertilisation (IVF)

IVF is a well-established method used to assist pregnancy by fertilising eggs and sperm in a laboratory setting. Surplus embryos created during this process can be utilised to procure embryonic stem cells. The intact donated embryos produced by IVF for research are cultured to the blastocyst stage. When the inner cell mass is formed, the inner cell masses are isolated from the blastocyst and disaggregated to obtain individual blastomeres which were then plated on a feeder layer and in a cultured medium. This method allows for the creation of stem cells that can be studied and potentially used in clinical applications (Sills et al., 2005).

Despite these advantages, stem cells derived from IVF-created embryos are not necessarily compatible to potential recipients. Without having certainty of its histocompatibility, transplantation therapies could never be a reality. An immunosuppressive drug is needed to prevent immune rejection or any severe post-transplantation effects. Furthermore, there are substantial ethical dilemmas attached to this technique; the destruction of human embryos, women being used to produce oocytes for research, women having to undergo the painful process of ovarian hyperstimulation, and the constant need to replace a scarce supply of oocytes.

Somatic cell nuclear transfer (SCNT)

SCNT is a cloning technique that has captured attention due to its role in producing Dolly the sheep, the first cloned mammal. This method involves transferring the nucleus of a somatic cell into an enucleated egg, forming an embryo. As an alternative to human pluripotent stem cells derived from IVF-created embryos, this technique generates stem cells that are compatible with the recipient avoiding immune rejection problem (Wakayama et al., 2001; Wilmut et al., 2002). However, this breakthrough met with support as well as ethical criticism. It is argued that allowing and encouraging this therapeutic technique will one day provide an opportunity for unethical exploitation of human cells, "a slippery slope" argumentation—it might open the door to the activity of human reproductive cloning. After the breaking news was announced, human reproductive cloning was banned across the globe in consensus. This decision does not put this technique to its end. It has been adapted to research for the medical benefits of humankind, later known as "therapeutic cloning" and it is allowed in some jurisdictions.

Altered nuclear transfer (ANT)

This innovative technique entails modifying the DNA of a somatic cell nucleus before transferring it into an enucleated egg. The result is a non-viable embryo that can still yield pluripotent stem cells while addressing certain ethical concerns associated with embryonic stem cells. Hurlbut articulates that this technique is developed with proper consultation with leading scientists, moral philosophers, and religious authorities without having to deal with the most disputatious exploitation, which is the destruction of human embryos. There is no destruction of embryos involved as there is no creation of viable human embryos. The generated ANT hybrid entity lacks the characteristics and capability of an organism and therefore, the destruction of this altered entity is not similar to the destruction of the unaltered embryo that is complete with functional structures and dynamic character of a potential organism (Hurlbut, 2005; Tam & Rossant, 2003). Notwithstanding this beneficial manipulation, it is disputable as to whether this early interference at the molecular level is safe and whether it will not cause any undesirable consequences down the line. As with the case of IVF, SCNT and other techniques that use oocytes, ANT is also facing the same issue of the need for numerous oocytes but having to involve oocyte donors in a complicated and risky stimulated ovulation process.

Induced pluripotency reprogramming

The groundbreaking discovery of induced pluripotent stem cells (iPSCs) involves reprogramming adult somatic cells to revert to an undifferentiated pluripotent state, effectively mimicking the properties of embryonic stem cells. This method has revolutionised stem cell research and earned researchers the Nobel Prize for its contribution to therapeutic applications (Evans & Kaufman, 1981; Takahashi et al., 2007; Yamanaka, 2012). It is highly possible for scientists to generate patient- and disease-specific pluripotent stem cells without having to worry about immune compatibility issues. However, there are concerns raised on the safety of using retroviruses in the reprogramming process and the minor genetic alterations or epigenetic alterations that are required for establishing iPSCs.

Parthenogenesis

Parthenogenesis refers to the development of embryos from unfertilised eggs activated through electric, chemical, or mechanical stimuli. This technique can generate stem cells without the ethical concerns surrounding fertilisation (Brevini & Gandolfi, 2008; Rougier & Werb, 2001). With the absence of DNA from the paternal cell, the egg undergoes development forming a clone of the maternal cell, thus causing abnormal development and giving rise to incomplete embryo-like structure unable to form an organism. Since the genomic imprinting is fully inherited from maternal cells, unlike SCNT, parthenogenetically derived stem cells are strictly compatible with oocyte donors. The use of parthenogenesis has been proposed as another possible alternative to procure embryonic stem cells. Nevertheless, an enormous number of oocytes are required for scientists to advance the existing basic research and the stem cells obtained are likely to benefit female rather than both gender counterparts. It may not be useful especially to develop universal therapy or specific therapy to treat Y chromosomes-linked disorders.

Blastomere extraction

This technique is conceptually based on the preimplantation genetic diagnosis that has been performed to screen embryo genomics before pregnancy commences. It begins with the creation of embryos through IVF then at a certain stage of blastocyst development; one or two blastomeres are extracted from the blastocyst to be used in generating stem cell lines without interfering with the potential development of the blastocyst. The blastocyst will be then transferred into the uterus for further development to result in a healthy pregnancy. This method aims to derive stem cells while preserving the potential for successful embryo development (Chung et al., 2006; Klimanskaya et al., 2006). However, there is a concern that the removal of blastomere in this early stage of embryonic development might significantly impact the reproductive competence of the embryo. Nevertheless, the rate of deriving human embryonic stem cells using this technique is quite low since only one or two blastomeres can be separated from human embryos at one time.

1.4 The accelerating horizon of hSCR

The landscape of biomedical science has undergone a monumental transformation over the past few decades, primarily driven by significant breakthroughs in hSCR. The seminal work by Ian Wilmut and his team in 1997, which resulted in the cloning of Dolly the sheep, set a precedent for cellular manipulation and regeneration. Following this, James Thomson's laboratory in 1998 successfully isolated hESCs, a feat that would unveil the remarkable potential of these cells to differentiate into various specialised cell types for regenerative therapies. The field took another ground-breaking leap forward with Shinya Yamanaka's discovery in 2007, which demonstrated that somatic cells could be reprogrammed to a pluripotent state, giving rise to induced pluripotent stem cells (iPSCs) (Schnieke et al., 1997; Takahashi et al., 2007; Thomson et al., 1998; Wilmut et al., 2007).

These breakthroughs have positioned hSCR as one of the most rapidly progressing and pivotal technologies in contemporary science. Scholars have noted its emergence as "one of the most high-profile and promising areas of 21st-century science" (Huang et al., 2013). The implications of these advancements stretch far beyond scientific curiosity; they represent a potential revolution in medical intervention. Stem cell research is now frequently discussed in the context of other groundbreaking technologies such as whole genome sequencing, biomarkers, gene therapy, and nanotechnology, underscoring its importance at the forefront of modern medicine (Khoury, 1997; Sahoo et al., 2017).

Scientists globally recognise the revolutionary potential of hSCR, particularly in treating degenerative diseases that remain largely incurable through conventional medical procedures. Conditions like neurodegenerative diseases, certain types of heart disease, and chronic degenerative conditions impose severe limitations in current therapeutic options, prompting urgent calls for innovative solutions (Banerjee et al., 2011; Daley & Scadden, 2008; Lodi et al., 2011; Panizzo, 2011; Uccelli & Prockop, 2010; Wagers, 2012). As emphasised by Daley (2012), the ageing global population requires advanced therapeutic approaches to manage ailments that no longer solely rely on drugs for a cure, thus highlighting the critical need for novel cell therapies that represent major frontiers in medical science.

1.5 Clinical applications: exploring the potentials of human embryonic stem cells

Human embryonic stem cells (hESCs) have emerged as a cornerstone of regenerative medicine, owing to their unique ability to proliferate indefinitely and differentiate into virtually any cell type within the human body. This remarkable property provides unprecedented access to human tissues, facilitating a deeper understanding of tissue differentiation and function. As researchers delve into the complexities of hESCs, they uncover potential pathways for enhancing drug safety and efficacy, marking the advent of a new era in pharmaceutical development.

1.5.1 Revolutionary implications for drug discovery

One of the most promising applications of hESCs lies in their utility for drug discovery (Rolletschek et al., 2004). By leveraging the capacity of hESCs to differentiate into specific cell types, scientists can create cellular models that closely mimic human physiology. For instance, human embryonic stem cell-derived heart cells have proven invaluable in assessing the safety of new drugs before they enter clinical trials (He et al., 2003). Such models allow researchers to identify potential toxicities or adverse effects early in the drug development process, significantly reducing the risks associated with human testing. The pharmaceutical industry has taken a keen interest in the potential of hESCs, recognising their immense value in drug screening processes (Baker, 2010). For instance, in the United Kingdom, a public-private consortium known as "Stem Cells for Safer Medicine" has been established with the ambition of developing a comprehensive bank of human cell lines sourced from hESCs for drug discovery. This initiative signifies a collaborative effort to harness the power of hESCs in developing safer therapeutic agents, efficiently accelerating the discovery process, and enhancing treatment outcomes.

In addition, the introduction of iPSCs has revolutionised not only the potential for regenerative therapies but also opened new avenues for drug discovery and development. The ability to generate patient-specific stem cells from somatic cells allows researchers to create disease models in vitro, thereby facilitating the exploration of disease mechanisms and enabling drug screening tailored to individual patient profiles (Ebert & Svendsen, 2010; Ellis & Bhatia, 2011; Grskovic et al., 2011; Inoue & Yamanaka, 2011). This innovative approach has garnered attention for its implications in personalising medicine, as it provides researchers with tools to identify potential drug candidates that could lead to more effective treatment options.

1.5.2 Breakthroughs in cancer treatment and blood production

Beyond drug discovery, hESCs have shown promising benefits in diverse areas of medical research. In a notable 2005 study, researchers at the University of Minnesota successfully generated "natural killer" cells from hESCs, demonstrating their capacity to target and destroy cancer cells (Knorr et al., 2013). This breakthrough illustrates the potential for hESC-derived cells to take on specific therapeutic roles, paving the way for innovative cancer treatments. Recent advancements have also seen scientists in the United Kingdom turning hESCs into red blood cells, a significant achievement aimed at addressing the persistent challenge of blood shortages for transfusions (Connor, 2010). Such breakthroughs underscore the versatility of hESCs and their potential to contribute to critical medical needs that affect countless individuals.

1.5.3 Understanding stem cells and disease mechanisms

Despite their vast potential, the efficient utilisation of hESCs is hindered by current limitations in understanding human embryonic development. Ongoing research aims to unravel the intricacies of hESC behaviour, particularly their self-renewal and growth regulation. Researchers at the University of Edinburgh have demonstrated that hESCs are not a homogenous cell type as previously believed. Instead, they encompass a variety of cells that can differentiate into specific lineages by responding to signals from their embryonic environment (Canham et al., 2010). This ability to switch between precursor states is fundamental to their versatility in generating diverse tissue types.

Research leveraging hESCs further illuminates disease mechanisms, serving as a powerful platform for understanding genetic disorders. A notable study focused on Down syndrome (trisomy 21) (Bhattacharyya & Svendsen, 2003), exploring how genetic errors during embryonic development can lead to severe health complications such as heart disease, leukaemia, and Alzheimer's disease. By employing hESC models, scientists can elucidate the underlying developmental mechanisms that contribute to these conditions, facilitating targeted intervention strategies in the future. Moreover, the establishment of new hESC lines from embryos with genetic disorders provides a rich *in vitro* model for investigating the ramifications of genetic mutations on cell proliferation and differentiation (Verlinsky et al., 2005). This approach opens avenues for potential treatments for pancreatic and heart diseases, reinforcing the significance of hESC research in addressing some of modern medicine's most pressing challenges (Bonner-Weir & Weir, 2005).

1.5.4 The global stem cell race

The landmark discoveries of the late 20th and early 21st centuries have catalysed a wave of research and development that holds for successful outcomes in treating complex degenerative diseases through stem cell therapies and this development has introduced a new paradigm in medical practice and reshaped our understanding of health and disease. One would argue that the trajectory of human stem cell research and potential stem cell-based therapy is indicative of a broader shift towards a future where regenerative and personalised medicine may become the norm.

Such promising and potential benefits of hSCR have not gone unnoticed, leading to enthusiastic engagement from international scientific communities. Countries around the world have actively joined in the so-called "stem cell race", with numerous nations prioritising stem cell research as a key area of investment and focus (Löser et al., 2010; Telegraph, 2003). This global movement is marked by a surge in scientific publications and collaborative efforts, indicating a shared commitment to advancing the field further. Reports have noted that "more nations are joining the human embryonic stem cell research (hESC) "race" by aggressively publishing in peer-reviewed journals", underscoring the urgency and vigour of research initiatives in this critical area (DeRouen et al., 2012, p. 2).

1.6 Conclusion

As previously shown, stem cells signify an extraordinary frontier in biological science and regenerative medicine; noted for their exceptional ability to self-renew and differentiate into a wide variety of specialised cell types. Their classification into totipotent, pluripotent, and multipotent types underscores not only their diverse potential but also their critical roles in development, health, and disease. Totipotent stem cells, the pioneers of life, give rise to all cell types essential for a functional organism. As development advances, the spotlight shifts to pluripotent stem cells, which are pivotal in regenerative therapies, while multipotent stem cells play crucial roles within specific adult tissues.

Among these, human embryonic stem cells (hESCs) stand out due to their unparalleled pluripotency, often regarded as the gold standard in stem cell research. Their potential to address a wide range of medical conditions, ranging from neurodegenerative diseases to blood-related disorders, and this marks them as vital for future therapeutic advancements. Furthermore, hESCs hold promise in drug discovery, offering platforms to model diseases, screen drug candidates, and develop personalised therapeutic strategies tailored to individual patient profiles.

As the global scientific community engages in what is often referred to as the "stem cell race", this collaborative effort fosters unprecedented growth and innovation within the field. This momentum highlights the urgent need for effective treatments for conditions that currently lack viable solutions, particularly given the global population ageing. Despite the myriad potential medical benefits associated with hESC research, the ethical implications surrounding their derivation cannot be ignored. The process of obtaining hESCs invariably involves the destruction of human embryos, raising profound moral questions.

The discourse surrounding hESCs therefore highlights the delicate balance between advancing medical knowledge and addressing the ethical dilemmas inherent in manipulating human life. The next chapter will delve deeper into critical issues regarding the moral status of human embryos, exploring various religious responses to this complex topic. It will also examine the ethical implications of using human embryos in research, shedding light on the diverse perspectives and arguments that inform this ongoing debate.

References

Arney, K. (2008, December 17). Tracking down bowel cancer stem cells. Cancer Research UK. https://news.cancerresearchuk.org/2008/12/17/tracking-down-bowel-cancer-stem-cells/

Baker, M. (2010). Testing time for stem cells. *Nature*, *463*(7282), 719. https://doi.org/10.1038/463719a

Banerjee, S., Williamson, D., Habib, N., Gordon, M., & Chataway, J. (2011). Human stem cell therapy in ischaemic stroke: A review. *Age and Ageing*, *40*(1), 7–13.

Barker, N., Ridgway, R. A., van Es, J. H., van de Wetering, M., Begthel, H., van den Born, M., Danenberg, E., Clarke, A. R., Sansom, O. J., & Clevers, H. (2009). Crypt stem cells as the cells-of-origin of intestinal cancer. *Nature*, *457*(7229), 608–611. https://doi.org/10.1038/nature07602

Bhattacharyya, A., & Svendsen, C. (2003). Human neural stem cells: A new tool for studying cortical development in Down's syndrome. *Genes, Brain and Behavior*, *2*(3), 179–186.

Bonner-Weir, S., & Weir, G. C. (2005). New sources of pancreatic β-cells. *Nature Biotechnology*, *23*(7), 857–861.

Brevini, T., & Gandolfi, F. (2008). Parthenotes as a source of embryonic stem cells. *Cell Proliferation*, *41*, 20–30.

Campbell, N. A., & Reece, J. B. (2005). *Biology*. Pearson, Benjamin Cummings. https://books.google.com.my/books?id=0jbm8J7VW0AC

Canham, M. A., Sharov, A. A., Ko, M. S., & Brickman, J. M. (2010). Functional heterogeneity of embryonic stem cells revealed through translational amplification of an early endodermal transcript. *PLoS Biology*, *8*(5), e1000379.

Caulfield, T., Rachul, C., & Zarzeczny, A. (2012). The evolution of policy issues in stem cell research: An international survey. *Stem Cell Reviews and Reports*, *8*, 1037–1042.

Chung, Y., Klimanskaya, I., Becker, S., Marh, J., Lu, S.-J., Johnson, J., Meisner, L., & Lanza, R. (2006). Embryonic and extraembryonic stem cell lines derived from single mouse blastomeres. *Nature*, *439*(7073), 216–219. https://www.nature.com/articles/nature04277.pdf

Connor, S. (2010, August 16). Scientific breakthrough as red blood cells are made from IVF embryos. The Independent. https://www.independent.co.uk/news/science/scientific-breakthrough-as-red-blood-cells-are-made-from-ivf-embryos-2053637.html

Crook, J. M., Peura, T. T., Kravets, L., Bosman, A. G., Buzzard, J. J., Horne, R., Hentze, H., Dunn, N. R., Zweigerdt, R., & Chua, F. (2007). The generation of six clinical-grade human embryonic stem cell lines. *Cell Stem Cell*, *1*(5), 490–494.

Daley, G. Q. (2012). The promise and perils of stem cell therapeutics. *Cell Stem Cell*, *10*(6), 740–749.

Daley, G. Q., & Scadden, D. T. (2008). Prospects for stem cell-based therapy. *Cell*, *132*(4), 544–548.

DeRouen, M. C., McCormick, J. B., Owen-Smith, J., & Scott, C. T. (2012). The race is on: Human embryonic stem cell research goes global. *Stem Cell Reviews and Reports*, *8*, 1043–1047.

Ebert, A. D., & Svendsen, C. N. (2010). Human stem cells and drug screening: Opportunities and challenges. *Nature Reviews Drug Discovery*, *9*(5), 367–372.

Ellis, J., & Bhatia, M. (2011). iPSC technology: Platform for drug discovery. *Clinical Pharmacology & Therapeutics*, *89*(5), 639–641.

EuroStemCell. An introduction to stem cells. https://www.eurostemcell.org

Evans, M. J., & Kaufman, M. H. (1981). Establishment in culture of pluripotential cells from mouse embryos. *Nature*, *292*(5819), 154–156.

Firlej, V., Barraud-Lange, V., & Fouchet, P. (2012). Stem cell therapy for male infertility takes a step forward. *Cell Stem Cell*, *11*(5), 585–586.

Gawrylewski, A. (2008, June 13). Embryonic stem cells still gold standard. The Scientist. https://www.the-scientist.com/embryonic-stem-cells-still-gold-standard-5051

Grskovic, M., Javaherian, A., Strulovici, B., & Daley, G. Q. (2011). Induced pluripotent stem cells—Opportunities for disease modelling and drug discovery. *Nature Reviews Drug Discovery*, *10*(12), 915–929.

He, J.-Q., Ma, Y., Lee, Y., Thomson, J. A., & Kamp, T. J. (2003). Human embryonic stem cells develop into multiple types of cardiac myocytes: Action potential characterization. *Circulation Research*, *93*(1), 32–39.

Heng, B. C., Richards, M., Shu, Y., & Gribbon, P. (2009). Induced pluripotent stem cells: A new tool for toxicology screening? *Archives of Toxicology*, *83*, 641–644.

Huang, Y., He, K., & Wang, X. (2013). Rapid prototyping of a hybrid hierarchical polyurethane-cell/hydrogel construct for regenerative medicine. *Materials Science and Engineering: C*, *33*(6), 3220–3229.

Hurlbut, W. B. (2005). Altered nuclear transfer as a morally acceptable means for the procurement of human embryonic stem cells. *Perspectives in Biology and Medicine*, *48*(2), 211–228.

Inoue, H., & Yamanaka, S. (2011). The use of induced pluripotent stem cells in drug development. *Clinical Pharmacology & Therapeutics*, *89*(5), 655–661.

Isasi, R. M., & Knoppers, B. M. (2006). Beyond the permissibility of embryonic and stem cell research: Substantive requirements and procedural safeguards. *Human Reproduction*, *21*(10), 2474–2481. https://doi.org/10.1093/humrep/del235

Khoury, M. J. (1997). Genetic epidemiology and the future of disease prevention and public health. *Epidemiologic Reviews*, *19*(1), 175–180.

Klimanskaya, I., Chung, Y., Becker, S., Lu, S.-J., & Lanza, R. (2006). Human embryonic stem cell lines derived from single blastomeres. *Nature*, *444*(7118), 481–485. https://www.nature.com/articles/nature05142

Knorr, D. A., Ni, Z., Hermanson, D., Hexum, M. K., Bendzick, L., Cooper, L. J., Lee, D. A., & Kaufman, D. S. (2013). Clinical-scale derivation of natural killer cells from human pluripotent stem cells for cancer therapy. *Stem Cells Translational Medicine*, *2*(4), 274–283. https://doi.org/10.5966/sctm.2012-0084

Lodi, D., Iannitti, T., & Palmieri, B. (2011). Stem cells in clinical practice: Applications and warnings. *Journal of Experimental & Clinical Cancer Research*, *30*, 1–20.

Löser, P., Schirm, J., Guhr, A., Wobus, A. M., & Kurtz, A. (2010). Human embryonic stem cell lines and their use in international research. *Stem Cells*, *28*(2), 240–246.

Panizzo, R. (2011, September 26). Britain trials embryonic stem cells as treatment for blindness. BioNews. https://www.progress.org.uk/britain-trials-embryonic-stem-cells-as-treatment-for-blindness/

Rolletschek, A., Blyszczuk, P., & Wobus, A. M. (2004). Embryonic stem cell-derived cardiac, neuronal and pancreatic cells as model systems to study toxicological effects. *Toxicology Letters*, *149*(1–3), 361–369.

Rougier, N., & Werb, Z. (2001). Minireview: Parthenogenesis in mammals. *Molecular Reproduction and Development*, *59*(4), 468–474.

Sahoo, S., Parveen, S., & Panda, J. (2017). The present and future of nanotechnology in human health care. *Nanomedicine in Cancer*, *3*, 775–806.

Scadden, D., & Srivastava, A. (2012). Advancing stem cell biology toward stem cell therapeutics. *Cell Stem Cell*, *10*(2), 149–150. https://doi.org/10.1016/j.stem.2012.01.010

Schnieke, A., McShir, J., Kind, A., Campbell, K., & Wilmut, I. (1997). Viable offspring derived from fetal and adult mammalian cells. *American Journal of Ophthalmology*, *2*(124), 276.

Sills, E. S., Takeuchi, T., Tanaka, N., Neri, Q. V., & Palermo, G. D. (2005). Identification and isolation of embryonic stem cells in reproductive endocrinology: Theoretical protocols for conservation of human embryos derived from in vitro fertilization. *Theoretical Biology and Medical Modelling*, *2*, 1–8.

Takahashi, K., Tanabe, K., Ohnuki, M., Narita, M., Ichisaka, T., Tomoda, K., & Yamanaka, S. (2007). Induction of pluripotent stem cells from adult human fibroblasts by defined factors. *Cell, 131*(5), 861–872.

Tam, P. P., & Rossant, J. (2003). Mouse embryonic chimeras: Tools for studying mammalian development. *Development, 130*, 6155–6163.

Telegraph, T. (2003, August 20). British 'rivals' lead way in stem cell race. https://www.telegraph.co.uk/news/science/science-news/3311703/British--rivals-lead-way-in-stem-cell-race.html?ICID=continue_without_subscribing_reg_first

Thomson, J. A., Itskovitz-Eldor, J., Shapiro, S. S., Waknitz, M. A., Swiergiel, J. J., Marshall, V. S., & Jones, J. M. (1998). Embryonic stem cell lines derived from human blastocysts. *Science, 282*(5391), 1145–1147.

Uccelli, A., & Prockop, D. J. (2010). Why should mesenchymal stem cells (MSCs) cure autoimmune diseases? *Current Opinion in Immunology, 22*(6), 768–774.

Verlinsky, Y., Strelchenko, N., Kukharenko, V., Rechitsky, S., Verlinsky, O., Galat, V., & Kuliev, A. (2005). Human embryonic stem cell lines with genetic disorders. *Reproductive Biomedicine Online, 10*(1), 105–110.

Wagers, A. J. (2012). The stem cell niche in regenerative medicine. *Cell Stem Cell, 10*(4), 362–369.

Wakayama, T., Tabar, V., Rodriguez, I., Perry, A. C., Studer, L., & Mombaerts, P. (2001). Differentiation of embryonic stem cell lines generated from adult somatic cells by nuclear transfer. *Science, 292*(5517), 740–743.

Wilmut, I., Beaujean, N., De Sousa, P., Dinnyes, A., King, T., Paterson, L., Wells, D., & Young, L. (2002). Somatic cell nuclear transfer. *Nature, 419*(6907), 583–587.

Wilmut, I., Schnieke, A., McWhir, J., Kind, A., & Campbell, K. (2007). Viable offspring derived from fetal and adult mammalian cells. *Cloning and Stem Cells, 9*(1), 3–7.

Yamanaka, S. (2012). Induced pluripotent stem cells: Past, present, and future. *Cell Stem Cell, 10*(6), 678–684.

2 The controversial issues of human embryos

2.1 Introduction

This chapter discusses the ethical issues posed by human stem cell research and therapy. The focus is largely given to the controversial issue of the use of human embryos for research purposes, which has led to the complex debate on whether human embryos have the same moral status as human persons. It is a contentious issue that sits at the crossroads of ethics, religion, and scientific advancement. As nations grapple with the implications of biotechnological progress, the perspectives of diverse religious traditions become increasingly significant, particularly in multicultural contexts like Malaysia, where Islam, Christianity, Hinduism, and Buddhism coexist. In these communities, beliefs about the sanctity of life, the definition of personhood, and the ethical boundaries of scientific inquiry shape public opinion and influence policy decisions.

In addressing the complex multifaceted nature of the moral and regulatory debate surrounding human embryos in the context of biomedical research, this chapter highlights the "14-day rule", a pragmatic approach that seeks to balance the pursuit of scientific knowledge with ethical considerations. This guiding rule, which restricts research on human embryos to the first 14 days of development, reflects an attempt to address the ethical concerns surrounding ensoulment and the potential for consciousness. However, as the understanding of embryology grows, and given the medical need to find cures for incurable diseases, questions remain about the ongoing relevance and adequacy of this regulation. Additionally, the chapter provides a brief overview of issues related to egg donations for stem cell research, exploring the ethical implications of this practice as well as the rise of unproven and often poorly regulated "stem cell therapies" that also raise serious ethical concerns. However, a comprehensive examination of these issues falls outside the scope of this book.

Through an examination of these critical themes, this chapter aims to foster a deeper understanding of the ethical landscape surrounding human embryos in research, highlighting the importance of dialogue among diverse religious and cultural perspectives in shaping a responsible approach to biomedicine in Malaysia and beyond.

DOI: 10.4324/9781003583479-2

2.2 Moral status of human embryos

The moral status of human embryos is a deeply polarising issue, triggering impassioned debates that intersect ethical philosophy, religious doctrine, and scientific inquiry. At the heart of this debate lies a fundamental question: when does human life begin, and what implications does this have for how we view the status of human embryos and their use in the context of research and medicine? This controversy touches the core of human experience, revealing the profound implications of our beliefs regarding life, personhood, and the ethics of scientific progress.

2.2.1 Fundamental questions of life and personhood

When does human life begin? This inquiry into the origins of personhood shapes not only individual beliefs but also public policy and ethical standards. Various perspectives exist on this topic, each offering distinct criteria for determining personhood. This chapter explores multiple viewpoints, including the virtue of nature, the virtue of potential, viability, sentience, birth, and the concepts of gradualism, relationality, and precautionary principle. Each perspective carries distinct implications on the permissibility of the use of human embryos for research purposes.

Full moral status

FOETUS AS A PERSON BY VIRTUE OF ITS NATURE

At the moment of conception, a sperm and an egg merge to form a zygote—an entity with a unique genetic identity. Proponents of this view argue that from this instant, the zygote possesses the inherent characteristics that define it as a person. Beckwith (2006, p. 182) articulates this notion by stating, "at conception, a whole human being, with its own genome, comes into existence, needing only food, water, shelter, oxygen, and a congenial environment in which to interact". The argument emphasises that the entire genetic makeup is established at conception, laying the foundation for future growth and development. Additionally, Kaczor (2005, p. 50) elaborates on this perspective by asserting that "a human embryo is properly classified as an individual human being rather than a collection of human cells, a member of the kind Homo sapiens rather than simply a 'heap' of human cells of human origin". He stresses that while skin cells are component parts of a human being, they lack the intrinsic capability to develop into a complete human organism. In contrast, the human embryo is a coordinated, living entity, marked by self-development towards maturity. Therefore, Kaczor concludes, if all human beings are recognised as persons, it logically follows that the human embryo should be afforded the same status.

FOETUS AS A PERSON BY VIRTUE OF ITS POTENTIAL

Another argument posits that the foetus deserves recognition as a person due to its potential to become a fully developed human being (Lu, 2011). This potential is inherent in the genetic constitution that exists from conception. Proponents argue that this capacity for development is sufficient to equate the embryo with a person, as it already possesses the biological blueprint necessary to grow into a complex individual. This view emphasises the value of potentiality: just as we recognise the importance of the potential of children and future generations, so too should we acknowledge the embryo as a valuable entity deserving of moral consideration.

THE PRECAUTIONARY PRINCIPLE

Given the uncertainty surrounding the exact moment at which personhood begins, many advocates of the view that life starts at conception argue for a precautionary approach (Beyleveld, 2018). They contend that there must be a specific moment in time when a human embryo transforms into a person. If this point is placed too late in gestation, we risk harming a moral being. Therefore, it is deemed safer to assume that life begins at conception. This perspective argues that, in the face of uncertainty, erring on the side of caution by granting personhood from conception is the most ethically responsible position, preventing any potential harm to what a moral individual may be.

Gradual moral status

THE GRADUALIST VIEW

Rejecting the binary categorisations of personhood, the gradualist view contends that there is no specific moment when a foetus becomes a person (Ehrich et al., 2007). Instead, it suggests a continuum of moral worth that increases as the foetus develops. This perspective implies that as the foetus acquires more characteristics associated with personhood—such as neurological development and physical capacity for life—greater moral respect is due. For instance, early-stage abortions may require less justification than those occurring later in pregnancy, as the foetus attains greater significance with its developmental progress.

A PERSON AT VIABILITY

One prominent view is that personhood begins at viability—typically recognised as around 22 weeks of gestation, when a foetus can survive outside the womb with medical assistance (Campo-Engelstein & Andaya, 2024; Kaczor, 2022). This perspective marks viability as a critical threshold because it signifies a point where the foetus has developed sufficient integrative functions characteristic of a human organism. At this stage, the foetus possesses the physiological capacity to maintain life independently from the mother, thus warranting recognition as a person. Advocates argue that this delineation underscores the transition from dependency to the potential for independent existence.

A PERSON AT SENTIENCE

Another influential perspective posits that a foetus becomes a person when it develops sentience, which is generally understood to occur between 20 to 24 weeks of gestation (Campo-Engelstein & Andaya, 2024). This view is rooted in the capacity for brain activity and self-awareness. Supporters argue that the emergence of sentience—as indicated by the development of brain activity—is significant because it signifies the ability to experience sensations and emotions. Dyson and Harris (2012, p. 63) emphasise a related point when they state, "They argue that the moral status of the embryo and indeed of any individual is determined by its possession of those features which make normal adult human individuals morally more important than sheep or goats or embryos". Thus, according to this view, life begins at the onset of meaningful brain activity, which serves as a marker for personhood.

Full moral status based on birth

A PERSON AT BIRTH

Reflecting current legal standards, the view that a foetus is not considered a person until birth is widely held. Under this perspective, personhood only emerges when the child is capable of biologically independent existence, which occurs when the foetus exits the womb. This transition allows the newborn to interact with the world outside the mother and become a member of the wider community. Consequently, the legal framework surrounding this position affirms that rights and protections are conferred only post-birth, where full legal personhood is recognised.

A PERSON POST-BIRTH

Philosophers Agata Sagan and Peter Singer advocate for a more radical stance: they argue that a foetus is not a person until it becomes a rational and self-conscious being (Sagan & Singer, 2007). Moreover, Singer suggests that newborns, lacking sufficient mental capacity and reasoning abilities, do not possess the same claim to life as fully developed persons. He controversially asserts that the life of a newborn may carry less intrinsic value than that of certain non-human animals, such as pigs or dogs. This perspective challenges traditional notions of personhood and posits that mental capacity and the ability to reason are requisite for establishing moral status.

Relationality moral status

THE RELATIONSHIP VIEW

An alternative approach emphasises the relational aspect of pregnancy, arguing that the status of the foetus cannot be discussed in isolation from its relationship with the mother (Campo-Engelstein & Andaya, 2024). This view posits that the mother and foetus are interconnected entities, whose lives and interests are deeply intertwined. Some scholars argue that this interconnectedness reflects the shared needs and reciprocal dependence of both parties. This perspective calls for an understanding of personhood that acknowledges the complexities of maternal-foetal relationships, highlighting the necessity of considering the mother's rights and the dynamics of their relationship in discussions of personhood.

2.2.2 The sanctity of life: religious doctrines and ethical considerations for embryo research

As previously illustrated, there are differing views from philosophical and moral arguments, on when human life begins. Proponents of the view that human life begins at conception argue that embryos possess intrinsic moral value and deserve protection from the moment of fertilisation. This moral argument emphasises the sanctity of life, which is profoundly valued and regarded as a cornerstone of various religious traditions.

In Islam, life is viewed as a divine gift from Allah, mandating its protection as a paramount moral duty. The Quran explicitly states, "Whosoever saves the life of one [human], it shall be as if he saved the life of all humankind" (Quran 5:32), underlining the significant weight placed on the sanctity of all human life, including that of the embryo, as Islamic scholars have interpreted this principle. Similarly, in Christianity, the sanctity of life is rooted in the belief that humanity is created in the image of God and likeness. This belief, supported by biblical texts such as Genesis 1:27, extends to the embryo, which is seen as inherently valuable from the moment of conception. The moral implications of destroying or manipulating embryos for research often raise serious ethical concerns for many Christians.

From a Buddhist perspective, the sanctity of life is anchored in the principles of compassion (karuṇā) and non-violence (ahimsa). The Dhammapada conveys the significance of life by stating, "All beings tremble before violence. All fear death. All beings appreciate life" (Dhammapada 129). This understanding prompts Buddhists to respect all living creatures, recognising their interconnection and the potential for enlightenment in every being. The ethical guidance in Buddhism stresses the repercussions of harming any life, thus promoting a culture of compassion. In Hinduism, the sanctity of life is similarly fundamental, relying on the concepts of *ahimsa* and the divine presence within all forms of life. Hindus view life as a manifestation of the divine (Brahman), reinforcing their commitment to non-violence as articulated in texts like the Mahabharata. Additionally, the belief in *karma* and reincarnation emphasises that one's actions directly impact future lives, heightening the importance of preserving life.

Despite the universal reverence for the sanctity of life expressed in these religious traditions, the application of this principle in the context of embryonic research presents complex challenges. While all religions advocate for the protection of life, the ethical considerations surrounding embryos can vary significantly. The subsequent sections illustrate these various ethical considerations.

2.3 Religious perspectives

2.3.1 Islam perspectives

Al Qurtubi once articulated that principles of ethics serve as the foundation of legislation in Islam (Haneef, 2006). This perspective is further supported by Al Qamihah, who asserts that Shari'ah is distinct from other legal systems in its ability to eliminate any duality between legal and ethical norms (Haneef, 2006). In addressing moral and ethical dilemmas, Islamic jurists refer to primary sources, which include: (i) the Quran, the Holy Book of Islam; (ii) the Sunna, the authentic traditions of the Prophet; (iii) Ijma, the consensus of scholarly opinion; and (iv) Qiyas, judgments derived through juristic analogy. The fact that the Quran is not the sole reference point, but rather one of several key sources, highlights the comprehensive nature of Islamic law and its integration of ethical principles.

The role of intention (niyyah) for the greater good

In Islamic ethics, the concept of *niyyah*, or intention, plays a critical role in evaluating the moral weight of an action (Rajabi & Khuzani, 2018). Therefore, the intention behind using embryos for research is a pivotal consideration within the Islamic framework. If the research aims for the greater good (utilitarianism) in finding cures for diseases, advancing medical knowledge, and ultimately alleviating suffering, this intention is morally justifiable. The pursuit of knowledge and the alleviation of human suffering are highly valued in Islam, leading some to support research that could yield significant medical benefits. However, if the intention behind the research is viewed as exploitative or lacking in respect for the embryo's potentiality, then such actions may be considered morally unacceptable.

The concept of public interest (maslahah)

Another important principle in Islamic ethics is the concept of *maslahah*, or welfare, which refers to the common good or public interest (Laludin, 2006). When assessing the use of human embryos for research, Islamic scholars may consider whether the potential benefits to society outweigh the ethical concerns associated with embryo manipulation. If research leads to significant advancements in healthcare that improve the quality of life and save lives, it may be viewed favourably from an Islamic perspective. This principle of *maslahah* allows for flexibility in ethical decision-making, encouraging considerations of current medical needs and societal benefits. As a result, some scholars would advocate for regulatory frameworks that ensure embryos are treated ethically, emphasising that any research undertaken should align with the ultimate goal of promoting human welfare without compromising Islamic values (Rahman et al., 2014).

From conception to ensoulment: Islamic views of embryonic life

The development of the human embryo is addressed in the Quran:

> And indeed, We created man from a quintessence of clay. Then we placed him as a small quantity of liquid (nutfa) in a safe lodging firmly established. Then we have fashioned the nutfa into something which hangs (alaqa). Then We made alaqa into a chewed lump of flesh (mudgha). And We made the mudgha into bones and clothed the bones with flesh. And then We brought it forth as another creation. So blessed the God, the best to create.
>
> (Quran 23: 12-14)

From this verse, many Muslim scholars interpret the term *nutfa* to refer to the blastocyst stage of development, *alaqa* to indicate the stage where the blastocyst attaches to the uterine wall, and *mudgha* to signify the stage where the lump of flesh resembles the early formation of somites (Nordin, 2006). Although these verses provide insight into embryonic development, the Quran does not specify the precise moment of ensoulment.

Many scholars argue that ensoulment occurs at a specific stage of development, as stated in the Quran; "and breathe into him of His spirit" (Quran 32:9). Each developmental phase is believed to last for 40 days, leading Muslim scholars to conclude that life begins at 120 days after conception. This belief is also supported with hadith literature, which provides further insight into the development of the human embryo where the Prophet Muhammad is reported to have stated that the angel breathes the spirit into the foetus at this stage. For instance, one hadith mentions:

> Verily your creation is on this wise. The constituents of one of you are collected for forty days in his mother's womb in the form of blood, after which it becomes a clot of blood in another period of forty days. Then it becomes a lump of flesh and forty days later Allah sends His angel to it with instructions concerning four things, so the angel writes down his livelihood, his death, his deeds, his fortune and misfortune.

Nonetheless, a minority of Islamic jurists believe that "ensoulment" takes place during the first 40 days of embryo development, suggesting the 40-day limit is a more cautious approach (Rispler-Chaim, 2006). Malaysian Muslims, who adhere to the Sunni school of thought, however, have accepted the resolution passed by the Muslim World League, which reflects the majority opinion that ensoulment occurs 120 days after conception (Nordin, 2011). This position is in line with a survey indicating that the majority of Muslim scholars do not regard embryos in their early stages of development as human persons (Eich, 2003).

Status of the embryo and personhood: progression from fertilisation to birth

Muslim scholars, however, do not determine the human status of an embryo solely based on the timing of ensoulment. First, some believe that an embryo attains its human status at conception, representing the most stringent view. Second, others argue that human status is granted when the embryo settles in the uterus wall. Third, there are those who believe that human status is conferred after ensoulment takes place at 40 days, and the latest at 120 days (Ghaly, 2012).

This illustrates the existing divergent views among Muslim scholars on the timing of when personhood begins and the status of an embryo, which significantly impacts the permissibility of human embryonic research. For instance, scholars who assert that human life begins at conception would oppose any research involving the destruction of embryos (Dabu, 2005). A strong position was articulated by the renowned medieval scholar, Abdul Hamid Al-Ghazali, who maintained that even if ensoulment occurs at a later stage, the embryo should still be regarded as a human being and thus should not be destroyed (Al-Hayani, 2008). Based on these differing perspectives, it can be concluded that achieving consensus among Muslim scholars on the interpretation of the Quran is nearly impossible.

Siddiqi (2002) argues that rather than debating whether an embryo qualifies as a human being and determining when it attains that status, the focus should be on distinguishing between an embryo in a petri dish and one in the womb. This distinction highlights the difference between actual life and potential life. An embryo in its natural environment has a genuine chance of survival, whereas an embryo in a petri dish has only a potential chance of survival, contingent upon being placed in a suitable environment. Therefore, an embryo created *in vitro* should not be regarded as a fully-fledged human being with all the corresponding rights. If these embryos were treated as full humans, it would prohibit the practice of producing them in excess and later destroying them. Mohamed (1995) further clarifies the distinction between *in vivo* and *in vitro* embryos by discussing their legal capacity and rights. There is no doubt that embryos acquire a right to live upon fertilisation; however, this right represents an incomplete legal capacity, which only becomes fully effective once the embryo develops into a foetus and is born. Early-stage human embryos possess less legal capacity compared to embryos at later stages of development and those that have been born.

Balancing ethics, religion, and science in embryonic research

Nevertheless, it is believed that human embryonic research is obligatory (fard kifayah) due to its significant potential to alleviate human disease and suffering, as highlighted earlier. On this basis, most Muslim scholars maintain that human embryonic research should be permitted, albeit under strict regulations. Siddiqi (2002) emphasises that such research should be heavily restricted, limited to surplus embryos created through *in vitro* fertilisation (IVF), with the full consent of donors being essential. Moreover, financial compensation for donors and the creation of new embryos are strictly prohibited. This perspective is fully incorporated in Malaysia's guidelines inspired by the National Fatwa Council. Many Muslim scholars accept the prevailing view that human embryonic research is permissible up to the 14th day post-fertilisation (Nordin, 2006). While some might wonder why the limit is set at 14 days instead of the 120 days associated with ensoulment, this choice has scientific justifications, which are discussed in the latter section of this chapter.

2.3.2 Christianity perspectives

Christian views on the moral status of the embryo vary among denominations. The Catholic Church, for instance, teaches unequivocally that "human life must be respected and protected absolutely from the moment of conception" (Catechism of the Catholic Church, 2270). This belief fosters a strong opposition to any research that involves the destruction of embryos, viewing it as a violation of the divine command to respect life. While the Catholic Church holds that personhood begins at conception, many Protestant groups may adopt a more nuanced stance. Some evangelical and mainline Protestant theologians assert that while embryos are deserving of moral consideration, the question of full personhood might be more complex.

Christian's traditional approach to defining the human embryo's status

In Islam, the Quran provides a clear account of embryonic development that Muslim scholars can reference. In contrast, Christian scriptures do not offer similar clarity on this topic (Peterson, 2003). However, several biblical passages touch upon the theme of creation and life that can help inform the discussion. For instance, Genesis 2:7 states, "Then the Lord God formed man from the dust of the ground, and breathed into his nostrils the breath of life; and the man became a living being". Psalm 139:13-16 further reflects on God's role in our formation: "For it was you who formed my inward parts; you knit me together in my mother's womb". Ecclesiastes 11:5 highlights the mystery of creation, stating, "Just as you do not know how the breath comes to the bones in the mother's womb, so you do not know the work of God, who makes everything". Finally, Jeremiah 1:5 emphasises God's awareness of us even before birth: "The Lord called me before I was born; while I was in my mother's womb, he named me" (Peterson, 2003). Despite the richness of these texts, as noted by Peterson, none of them explicitly address the timing of human existence in relation to embryonic development. Consequently, Christian scholars may find it challenging to rely solely on scripture to determine the moral status of the human embryo. This is because there are no biblical references or scriptures that provide definitive guidance on the timing of ensoulment (Davis, 2004; Foong, 2011).

Moreover, Christian tradition often distinguishes between "formed" and "unformed" bodies when determining the moment life begins. Throughout the early and medieval church, theologians held that ensoulment occurs when a body has developed within the womb. Before this formation, the life developing in the womb was regarded as "unformed" (Peterson, 2003). A pertinent reference can be found in the Septuagint translation of Exodus 21:22, which states,

> If anyone strikes a pregnant woman and she miscarries, then if the foetus is formed, the penalty is death; if, on the other hand, the foetus is not yet formed as a likeness of a human being, then the penalty is a fine.
>
> (Council)

This passage illustrates a distinction in punishments based on whether the life taken is classified as formed or unformed. If a formed body is killed, the penalty is "life for life", implying that a formed body possesses a soul or life. Conversely, if an unformed body is lost, the lesser punishment of a fine suggests it lacks a soul.

Contrasting Christian approaches to embryo research

According to Roman Catholic tradition, St. Thomas Aquinas believed that the soul entered the male foetus at 40 days and the female foetus at 90 days (Council). This distinction can be puzzling, especially since none of the aforementioned scriptures delineate between male and female foetuses. It is said that St. Thomas relied on "the best science available in his day", specifically the figures provided by Aristotle (Peterson, 2003). Consequently, one would argue that for those who subscribe to this view, would find the use of human embryos for research purposes to benefit humankind as morally acceptable.

In contrast, the contemporary Roman Catholic Church firmly opposes human embryonic research. This stance is reflected in a statement confirmed by the Magisterium of the Church, which asserts the following key points: (i) Based on a comprehensive biological analysis, the living human embryo is a distinct human subject from the moment of gamete union. From this point, it begins its own coordinated, continuous, and gradual development, such that it can no longer be regarded as simply a mass of cells; (ii) As a human individual, the embryo possesses the right to its own life. Moral theology has consistently taught that in situations involving uncertain third-party outcomes, the system of probabilism does not apply; (iii) Consequently, the ablation of the inner cell mass (ICM) of the blastocyst, which critically and irreparably damages the embryo and hinders its development, is deemed a gravely immoral act and is therefore gravely illicit; (iv) Moreover, no perceived good end, such as the use of stem cells for promising therapeutic treatments, can justify actions that are intrinsically wrong (Vita, 2000).

This statement clearly illustrates the Roman Catholic Church's absolutist stance against the use of human embryos for the benefit of human beings, asserting that the embryo is a human individual from the moment of conception. An empirical study indicated that adherents of the Catholic faith in Malaysia align with the Vatican's firm stance that human embryonic research is tantamount to infanticide as it involves the destruction of human embryos (Foong, 2011). However, it is noteworthy that some of the Roman Catholic members of the House of Lords in the United Kingdom shifted their perspective after observing a four-cell embryo in a laboratory (Warnock, 1987). They argued that embryos before 14 days of development should not receive full legal protection and proposed such entities be referred to as "pre-embryos" rather than embryos.

Less conservative Protestant churches view embryos as having potential human status, reflecting their gradual development from basic cells into actual human organisms. As a result, some embryo research may be permitted. The life of a human embryo is still considered sacred from its conception, however, the potential benefits of its use for research can be considered with some protections (Hug, 2006).

2.3.3 Buddhism perspectives

Basic teachings of Buddhism centre on the values of *karuna* or compassion, *prajnal* or knowledge, no-self, non-injury, and relief of suffering of sentient beings. Buddhism teaches the concept of reincarnation and rebirth but does not include the notion of ensoulment. The ultimate goal of a Buddhist is to attain enlightenment or awakening. Within Buddhism, perspectives on the contentious ethical issue of the use of human embryos for research purposes are deeply rooted in its core ethical principles, including the doctrines of *ahimsa* or non-harming, interdependence, and the impermanence of material existence (Harvey, 2008).

The principle of non-harming (ahimsa)

At the heart of Buddhist ethics lies the principle of non-harming, or *ahimsa*, which holds that one should avoid causing harm to any living being (Harvey, 2008). This foundational tenet influences Buddhist views on the moral status of human embryos. Many Buddhists would argue that embryos, despite being in the early stages of development, are potential sentient beings, and using them in research could be seen as a form of harm. The potentiality for life imbues embryos with a moral significance that must be respected. However, interpretations of *ahimsa* can vary. Some Buddhists may emphasise the importance of weighing the potential benefits of research, such as advancements in medical science and potential treatments for suffering, against the act of using embryos. This consequentialist/utilitarian approach allows for the consideration of the greater good that might arise from research, particularly if it could prevent harm and alleviate suffering for countless living beings. It can also be argued that *ahimsa*, which signifies non-violence towards sentient beings, does not apply to embryos, as they are considered potential sentient beings rather than sentients themselves. Therefore, one could assert that the principle of *ahimsa* is not violated in this context (Foong, 2011).

Interdependence and the connectedness of all life

Another significant concept in Buddhism is the doctrine of interdependence, which posits that all beings exist in relation to one another and that the actions of one can have far-reaching effects on others (Schlieter, 2022). This perspective encourages a holistic view of ethical issues, prompting Buddhists to consider how embryo research impacts not only the embryos themselves but also the broader web of life, including the potential future patients who could benefit from medical advancements derived from such research. By recognising the interconnectedness of all beings, some Buddhists may argue that the potential benefits of using human embryos for research can be justified. This perspective aligns with the concept of "enforced donor", which suggests that sacrificing (or donating) one's life for the benefit of another may not be inherently wrong in certain circumstances (Foong, 2011; Promta, 2004). Advances in regenerative medicine, stem cell research, and therapies for serious diseases might be viewed as opportunities to benefit many people by enhancing the quality of life and reducing suffering—an essential aim in Buddhist practice.

Impermanence, the nature of existence, and personhood

Buddhism teaches the concept of *anicca* or impermanence, which suggests that all phenomena are transient and subject to change. This understanding can inform views on the moral status of human embryos. From a Buddhist perspective, the material form is often seen as less significant than the flow of consciousness and the opportunities for future experiences. Therefore, the potential of an embryo to develop into a sentient being must be weighed against its current state as an undifferentiated entity. While some may argue that an embryo, as a potential future person, should be afforded the same moral consideration as a fully developed human being, others within the Buddhist community might contend that embryos cannot possess the same status as a person due to their lack of consciousness and self-awareness that a person would develop (Keown, 2017). This viewpoint emphasises the dynamic nature of life and suggests that the ethical implications of using embryos for research can be contextual and relative to their developmental stage.

Intention and compassionate action

The ethical dilemmas surrounding the use of human embryos in research highlight the need for intention and compassionate action, which is a fundamental aspect of Buddhist practice. Buddhists are encouraged to approach such issues not solely from a place of philosophical reasoning but also with the right intention and compassion for all involved. This includes considering the experiences of parents seeking treatment for infertility, individuals suffering from debilitating diseases, and the embryos themselves. In contemporary discussions, some Buddhist scholars advocate for ethical frameworks that prioritise intention and compassion, emphasising the importance of dialogue within the community to navigate the complexities of reproductive technologies and medical research. It was argued that in dealing with the ethical dilemmas of research involving human beings and human embryos, it would depend on the intention of the researchers and the use of his or her wisdom (Promta, 2004).

2.3.4 Hinduism perspectives

Hinduism is a polytheistic religion that believes in many gods. Its teachings aim to promote a fulfilling life, overcome suffering, and attain enlightenment. Hinduism and Buddhism share many similar philosophies. Among other beliefs, Hindus also subscribe to the concept of reincarnation and do not adhere to the notion of a specific timing for ensoulment. They believe *atman* or soul is eternal; it is the body that comes into existence and eventually perishes, while the soul endures indefinitely.

Hindu perspectives on the ethical considerations surrounding the use of human embryos in research are deeply intertwined with core beliefs about *atman* or soul, *moksha* or one's union with God, and *ahimsa* or the principle of non-harming of sentient beings (Bhanot, 2008).

The sacredness of atman or soul

A foundational belief in Hinduism is the sanctity of all life, which is deeply rooted in the concept of *ahimsa*, or non-violence. This principle obligates Hindus to avoid causing harm to any living being, including embryos. Many Hindus believe that life begins at conception (Jafari et al., 2008), as the embryo is seen as a vessel for the soul, which is believed to enter the body at this stage. Consequently, the use of embryos in research may be viewed as morally problematic, as it could be perceived as violating the sanctity of life by treating potential human beings as mere means to an end.

Moreover, the belief that each soul is on a journey through cycles of birth, death, and *samsara* or rebirth adds another layer to this perspective. Each embryo, holding the potential for future experiences and spiritual growth, is considered sacred. Thus, the destruction of embryos for research purposes can conflict with the Hindu understanding of the divine journey of the soul.

The concept of dharma and ethical duty

The concept of *dharma*, which refers to one's duty and ethical responsibilities, plays a crucial role in determining moral actions in Hindu teachings. Given the advancements in medical science, particularly in areas such as stem cell therapy and regenerative medicine, hold the promise of alleviating suffering and saving lives, some Hindus might argue that engaging in research that leads to the betterment of health and well-being aligns with a sense of *dharma*, especially if it results in reducing human suffering, and therefore cultivating the spiritual awareness to achieve *moksha* or liberation. This utilitarian view may lead to a nuanced stance where the potential benefits of research are considered alongside the inherent respect for life.

The role of intent in ethical considerations

The significance of *manas*, or mind, and *sankalpa* or intention in Hindu ethics cannot be overlooked. The moral weight of an action is considered closely tied to the intent behind it (Jafari et al., 2008). Research into human embryos may be viewed differently depending on the intentions of those conducting the research. If the intent is to advance knowledge and contribute to healing, some may argue that this is a noble pursuit and should be allowed. However, if the intent is perceived as exploitative or devoid of respect for life, it may be deemed unethical. Hindu teachings emphasise the journey towards *moksha,* which involves cultivating righteousness and compassion. Therefore, it is important for Hindus to approach embryo research with a framework that prioritises ethical integrity and compassion for all sentient beings involved, including potential future human beings.

2.4 The 14-day rule

As has been demonstrated in the preceding sections, it is difficult to determine the moral status of human embryos from both philosophical and religious discourses. When the Warnock Committee was introduced in the United Kingdom to determine whether scientific research on human embryos should be permitted, the Committee faced the challenge of addressing this moral debate. Not only the public in the United Kingdom are divided in their views on the moral status of human embryos, but the Committee itself also had disagreements on the matter. Nonetheless, the Committee in consensus believe that despite the uncertainty of its moral status, human embryos which are used for research should be provided with special protection under the law, however, the protection should not be absolute.

The Committee introduced the "14-day rule", as a pragmatic approach to address the contentious issue, whereby embryo research should only be permitted up to 14 days after fertilisation. This time limit element was suggested by Anne McLaren, a renowned developmental biologist, who observed that the central nervous system in humans begins to develop after the 14th day (Hogan, 2001). This was a moral compromise which the Committee thought would be pragmatically acceptable to all, especially to maintain public trust in researchers (Plomer, 2002). The Committee proposed the 14-day limit based on several considerations: the emergence of the primitive streak (a precursor to the nervous system), the capacity for embryonic development, and the philosophical concept that personhood has not yet been established at this stage.

Since then, this time limit has been adopted by various countries as a mechanism to control embryo research while balancing ethical considerations regarding potential human life. In addition, the Committee further put in place a clear limit to embryo research by recommending that embryo research should only be permitted under licence to help mitigate public fear of unethical conduct involving human embryos by unscrupulous scientists. However, not all jurisdictions, including Malaysia, that have adopted the 14-day rule also impose licencing requirements in their legal framework.

2.4.1 Is the 14-day rule still relevant?

It has been 44 years since the 14-day rule was first introduced by the Warnock Committee in the United Kingdom. It has been a cornerstone of ethical guidelines and legislative frameworks in regulating the use of human embryos for research, not only in the United Kingdom, but also in many other jurisdictions, including Australia, parts of the European Union, and Asia. However, as scientific advancements in reproductive technologies and genetic engineering progress, there is increasing debate within academic discourses regarding the continued relevance of this rule. This discussion encompasses ethical and scientific dimensions, raising questions about the appropriateness and implications of the 14-day limit in the context of contemporary human embryo research.

This question was raised when scientists reported in reputable journals namely *Nature* and *Nature Cell Biology* in 2016 that it is now possible to culture embryos beyond this time limit (Deglincerti et al., 2016; Shahbazi et al., 2016), and as a result, there is a pressure to extend the current limit to 28 days (Castelyn, 2020; Hyun et al., 2021; McCully, 2021). Since then many have argued that there might be a need to review the 14-day rule (Hurlbut et al., 2017) especially after more researchers have also reported the same discovery (Ma et al., 2019). It was also argued that when the 14-day rule was introduced, scientists were not able to culture human embryos close to the 14th day, and given the current scientific advancement, the current threshold is viewed as less reasonable compared to when it was first adopted.

Considering the new capabilities, many scientists contended that there is a need to reevaluate the existing ethical standards governing research that utilises human embryos. They proposed the extension of the time limit to allow them to study the developmental processes during gastrulation when the first primitive tissues form in embryos. This way, they could learn more about the development of the nervous system without any risk of neural connection being present and understand the early development of organs. It is also possible to have an advanced understanding of cell fate decisions during early embryonic development. Many studies have reported that many important events that take place during early embryogenesis, prior to the 14th day, are likely to have an impact on later development. If research work stops before the 14th day, it will be hard for scientists to ascertain the real significance of these important events.

They also could potentially understand the nature of some birth defects or developmental abnormalities (McCully, 2021). For instance, congenital heart disease is a condition caused by abnormal formation of the heart that occurs during foetal development. Currently, there is an effort to investigate heart formation in mice and similar research in humans would be possible and beneficial but such research is not possible due to the 14-day rule. Understanding embryo development could also be useful in improving the success rate of IVF procedures (Blackshaw & Rodger, 2021) whereby it can facilitate clinicians to predict which IVF-derived embryos would be likely to result in a successful pregnancy. By extending the time limit beyond the 14 days, would also enable scientists to learn more about the physiology of pregnancy beyond the 14th day, including the implantation process and the contributing factors of miscarriages. In addition, scientists have also argued that at 28 days after fertilisation, there will be no neural connections or sensory system being developed in the embryo and, therefore, it is impossible for it to experience sentience, pain, or suffering within this extended period of research (Appleby & Bredenoord, 2018).

Notwithstanding the promising benefits that the time extension will offer, there are opposing views against the extended time limit. It was argued that due to the onset of gastrulation signifies that the embryo is a distinct individual, and therefore, has a greater potential for personhood, the embryo acquires greater moral standing after the 14th day. In relation to the argument that it is crucial to find out the events that occur after the 14th day given the new capability in culturing embryos up to the 14th day, it was contended that such a research capability only materialised in 2016 and, therefore the current development is still in its infancy (Blackshaw & Rodger, 2021). Consequently, it can be argued that it is rather premature to extend the time limit when the current limit has not been fully exploited. In addition, there is a concern if the proposed extension to 28 days is accepted, this could be the beginning of a slide down the slippery slope towards an ever-increasing time window for research that uses human embryos. In addition, such an extension is precisely the type of slippery slope that was originally raised previously (Appleby & Bredenoord, 2018; Blackshaw & Rodger, 2021).

However, there is a concern about the relevance of the 14-day rule especially from scientific perspectives and due to new research advancements. There are critics who argue the arbitrary significance of the time limit that lacks a robust scientific foundation. For instance, Hyun et al. (2016) emphasise that advances in developmental biology challenge traditional notions of the "beginning of human life". They argue that defining moral status or personhood based solely on embryonic developmental milestones may not adequately account for the complexities of moral and ethical considerations in a rapidly changing scientific landscape. Also, it was contended that once an embryo passes the point where it can be successfully implanted, it loses its moral status of becoming a potential person and, therefore, there is no moral reason to extend the 14-day rule (Blackshaw & Rodger, 2021).

Scholars such as Darnovsky (2018) further contend that the 14-day rule fails to address the ethical implications of embryo manipulation techniques such as CRISPR gene editing and synthetic biology, which offers the potential for creating entities that do not fit neatly into the existing ethical paradigm surrounding human embryos. Additionally, the emergence of "organoids" (lab-grown tissues that simulate organ functions) has fuelled debates regarding human dignity and moral status. For example, how to differentiate the moral status between standard embryos and organoids as the new advancement causes difficulties in establishing boundaries between biological material worthy of ethical consideration (Mollaki, 2021). This ambiguity may call into question whether the 14-day rule can adequately address the implications of such scientific advancements.

This section has highlighted the potential implications of extended embryo culture for understanding embryonic development better. Such research suggests that the status and development of embryos may merit further ethical examination beyond the current rule, leading to calls for a reconsideration of the ethical boundaries of embryo research. As to whether the 14-day rule is still relevant, some argue that the reasoning behind the rule is still applicable (Blackshaw & Rodger, 2021). Nonetheless, the International Society for Stem Cell Research (ISSCR) has recommended potential exceptions to the 14-day limit under strict ethical oversight for research purposes that could advance scientific knowledge or therapeutic applications (ISSCR, 2021). However, this flexibility is often met with resistance. Many stakeholders, including advocacy groups, ethicists, and the public, hold strong convictions about the moral implications of embryo research, complicating the conversation surrounding the relevance of the 14-day rule (Matthews et al., 2021).

2.5 Egg donations for stem cell research

Egg donation for stem cell research presents significant opportunities for advancing medical science, particularly in regenerative medicine to develop therapies for various diseases. However, it also entails various physical and social harms that can affect donors and the wider community. Understanding these aspects is crucial for developing ethical guidelines and protective measures for those involved in the donation process.

2.5.1 Physical harm

Ovarian Hyperstimulation Syndrome (OHSS) represents one of the most significant physical risks associated with egg donation. It can arise from the hormonal stimulation necessary for egg retrieval, potentially leading to a range of complications that vary from mild abdominal discomfort to severe, life-threatening conditions. Studies indicate that women undergoing ovarian stimulation may experience severe OHSS, which can necessitate hospitalisation and lead to long-term health issues, including chronic pain and an increased risk of thrombosis.

The egg retrieval process itself is conducted under sedation and is considered a minor surgical procedure. While generally safe, this procedure carries inherent risks, including infection, bleeding, and potential damage to surrounding organs. Although serious adverse events are uncommon, they can have significant short- and long-term repercussions on women's health. In addition to physical risks, the hormonal treatments required for egg donation can also impact psychological well-being. Women may experience mood swings and heightened anxiety during the process, and emotional distress related to the physical changes. The high-stakes nature of egg donation can also raise concerns about the mental health of donors both during and after the donation experience (Jacxsens et al., 2024).

2.5.2 Social harm

The egg donation industry often faces criticism for its potential to exploit vulnerable populations and for the moral implications of treating human gametes as marketable commodities (Kenney & McGowan, 2014). Many egg donors are young women or college students who, driven by financial pressure or the allure of compensation, may overlook the associated risks of the donation process (Levine, 2011). This raises ethical concerns about informed consent and the adequacy of protection afforded to donors.

Moreover, egg donation can exacerbate existing socioeconomic inequalities. Wealthier individuals have the means to purchase donor eggs, while those from lower socioeconomic backgrounds may feel compelled to donate purely out of financial necessity. A number of studies highlight this disparity, indicating that economically disadvantaged donors often face ethical dilemmas when their financial needs compel them to take health risks that wealthier individuals can avoid (Gupta, 2012; Ikemoto, 2009; Nahman, 2011).

Additionally, donors from economically disadvantaged backgrounds may encounter stigma or social isolation, particularly in communities where egg donation is viewed negatively or is poorly understood. This stigma can result in feelings of shame and secrecy, profoundly impacting their social interactions. Furthermore, egg donation can complicate family dynamics and raise significant questions about identity and relationships. Donors may grapple with the knowledge that their eggs have contributed to the creation of children, leading to complex emotions regarding their biological role. Both donors and donor-conceived individuals may face identity challenges as they navigate these biological connections, complicating their understanding of self and family.

2.6 The unproven stem cell treatment

The emergence of unproven stem cell therapies has become a significant issue worldwide, raising concerns regarding patient safety, ethical standards, and the integrity of medical practices (Sipp, 2011). Unregulated clinics and entrepreneurs are increasingly marketing these therapies, often leveraging patients' hopes for cures to various medical conditions (Master et al., 2021).

This section briefly explores the types of unproven stem cell therapies being offered globally, the challenges associated with regulating these practices, particularly in developing nations, and the implications for public health.

2.6.1 Types of unproven stem cell therapies

Autologous stem cell transplants

One of the most common forms of unproven therapy involves the use of autologous stem cells—cells harvested from the patient's own body, often from adipose (fat) tissue or bone marrow. Clinics offer these treatments for a variety of conditions, including neurological disorders (like multiple sclerosis and Parkinson's disease), autoimmune diseases, and orthopaedic issues such as osteoarthritis. While the theory underlying their use is based on the regenerative potential of stem cells, there is a lack of rigorous evidence to support their efficacy for these indications (McLean et al., 2015).

Allogeneic stem cell therapies

These therapies involve the use of stem cells from a donor, typically cord blood or embryonic sources (Singh & McGuirk, 2016). Clinics sometimes market allogeneic stem cell treatments for a range of serious conditions, including chronic illnesses such as diabetes and even terminal diseases like cancer. However, many of these applications are not backed by scientifically validated data, leading to significant safety concerns (Dulak & Pecyna, 2023).

Combination therapies

Some therapies combine stem cell administration with other unproven interventions, such as the use of untested drugs or supplements, creating a convoluted treatment strategy that complicates the evaluation of safety and efficacy. The lack of transparency in these treatment protocols further blurs the lines for regulatory bodies tasked with overseeing them.

2.6.2 Difficulty in regulating unproven stem cell therapies

Regulatory frameworks for stem cell therapies vary significantly across the globe (Sipp et al., 2017). In developed countries like the United States, the Food and Drug Administration (FDA) plays a crucial role in overseeing stem cell practices, mandating rigorous testing before therapies can be marketed to the public. In contrast, many developing countries struggle with weak or non-existent regulatory systems, creating an environment where unproven therapies can proliferate without adequate oversight. For instance, Malaysia and several Southeast Asian nations lack comprehensive regulations governing the marketing and distribution of stem cell therapies, resulting in a surge of clinics offering questionable treatments (Bin Abdul Aziz et al., 2018; Sipp, 2009).

Compounding this issue is the rise of medical tourism, where patients travel abroad in search of affordable or experimental treatments that are often unavailable in their home countries (McMahon, 2014). This trend presents significant challenges for regulators both domestically and in destination countries. Home countries lose control over the health choices of their citizens, while destination countries face increased pressure on local health systems due to the influx of foreign patients seeking unregulated therapies.

Another critical concern is the lack of awareness among patients regarding the legitimacy and safety of stem cell therapies. Misinformation can spread rapidly, leading individuals to seek treatments from unregulated clinics without fully understanding the associated risks (Smith et al., 2020). Research indicates that many patients are susceptible to misleading advertising and often struggle to evaluate the scientific credibility of the therapies being offered. This vulnerability underscores the need for better education and awareness to help patients make informed decisions about their health.

2.6.3 Ethical concerns and challenges of unproven stem cell therapy in developing countries

Patient safety and exploitation

One of the primary ethical concerns surrounding unproven stem cell therapies is patient safety. Many clinics in developing countries offer treatments that have not undergone rigorous clinical trials, exposing patients to significant health risks. Unverified stem cell treatments can lead to severe complications, including tumour formation and infections. The lack of stringent regulatory frameworks means that patients may be vulnerable to exploitation by profit-driven practices that prioritise financial gain over patient welfare.

Informed consent

Informed consent is a cornerstone of ethical medical practice; however, in the context of unproven therapies, obtaining truly informed consent can be problematic. Patients may not receive comprehensive information about the lack of evidence supporting the treatment, potential risks, and realistic expectations for outcomes. Many patients seeking stem cell therapies offered by fraudulent providers might be misled about the efficacy and safety of these treatments, which undermines their ability to provide informed consent.

Regulatory and institutional frameworks

One of the most significant challenges in addressing the issue of unproven stem cell therapies in developing countries is the inadequacy of regulatory frameworks. Many countries, including Malaysia, lack comprehensive legislation and enforcement mechanisms to oversee stem cell therapy practices. In contrast, developed countries typically have established regulatory bodies, such as the Food and Drug Administration (FDA) in the United States, which can enforce standards for safety and efficacy. The limited regulatory capacity in developing nations often results in a "wild west" environment for medical practices, where unproven treatments flourish with minimal oversight.

Public awareness and education

Developing countries also face challenges in public awareness and education about stem cell therapies. Misinformation can spread rapidly, leading patients to pursue unproven treatments without fully understanding the risks involved. Many patients might lack adequate knowledge regarding stem cell research, making them susceptible to exploitation by unscrupulous clinics. In contrast, developed countries generally have greater access to educational resources that inform the public about the science of stem cell therapies and the importance of evidence-based treatments. This can be seen from the websites of regulators in developed countries that provide information for all relevant stakeholders including members of the public.

Research infrastructure

The capacity for conducting rigorous clinical research is often limited in developing countries. This lack of research infrastructure hinders the ability to generate high-quality evidence required to evaluate the safety and effectiveness of new treatments. While developed countries invest heavily in research and development, many developing nations struggle with insufficient funding and resources to support comprehensive clinical studies. This makes it difficult to establish standards of care and validate treatment efficacy, perpetuating the cycle of unregulated practices.

2.7 Conclusion

The moral status of human embryos is a complex issue that combines ethical, philosophical, and scientific discussions, centring around the critical question of when human life begins. Opinions vary widely: some consider a zygote a person from conception, while others adopt a gradualist view or define personhood based on various criteria such as potentiality or birth. Religious perspectives also play a significant role in this debate, as major faith traditions, like Islam, Christianity, Buddhism, and Hinduism, share a reverence for the sanctity of life but have differing interpretations regarding the use of embryos in research.

The emergence of the "14-day rule" has become a pivotal guideline within the ethical landscape of human embryonic research, serving as a compromise between advancing scientific inquiry and safeguarding moral considerations regarding embryonic life. By restricting research to the initial 14 days post-fertilisation, the rule acknowledges key developmental milestones while allowing essential scientific advancements. However, as scientific understanding and reproductive technologies evolve rapidly, the relevance of this rule is increasingly called into question, highlighting the need for ongoing ethical debate and possible re-evaluation of the established timeframe. Furthermore, the emergence of new techniques, such as gene editing and organoids, introduces critical ethical dilemmas that the 14-day rule may not fully address. Consequently, it is vital for ethical frameworks to adapt to these advancements and cultivate a regulatory environment that thoughtfully navigates the intersection of scientific progress, ethical integrity, and public opinion, thereby upholding the moral fabric of society alongside its scientific endeavours.

Similarly, egg donation for stem cell research presents a critical intersection of scientific advancement and ethical responsibility. While it holds significant promise for medical treatments, it poses notable risks to donors, such as Ovarian Hyperstimulation Syndrome and emotional distress. The potential for exploitation and socioeconomic disparities further complicates the issue, highlighting the need for strong ethical guidelines to ensure informed consent and equitable access. Additionally, the commercialisation of unproven stem cell-based therapies across the globe raises ethical concerns and poses significant global challenges that impact patient safety, ethical standards, and the integrity of medical practices. Patients often seek therapies in hopes of cures for various medical conditions, but the lack of rigorous evidence raises serious concerns. In developed countries, regulatory bodies like the FDA enforce strict rules; however, many developing nations do not have adequate regulatory framework, allowing dubious clinics to thrive without oversight. The situation is compounded by the rise of medical tourism, where patients travel to regions with fewer regulations, further complicating public health efforts.

References

Al-Hayani, F. A. (2008). Muslim perspectives on stem cell research and cloning. *Zygon*®, *43*(4), 783–795.

Appleby, J. B., & Bredenoord, A. L. (2018). Should the 14-day rule for embryo research become the 28-day rule? *EMBO Molecular Medicine*, *10*(9), e9437. https://pmc.ncbi.nlm.nih.gov/articles/PMC6127884/pdf/EMMM-10-e9437.pdf

Beckwith, F. J. (2006). Defending abortion philosophically: A review of David Boonin's a Defense of Abortion. *The Journal of Medicine and Philosophy*, *31*(2), 177–203.

Beyleveld, D. (2018). The moral and legal status of the human embryo. In *In vitro fertilisation in the 1990s* (pp. 247–260). Routledge.

Bhanot, A. (2008). *The ethics of stem cell research: A Hindu view*. Retrieved September 28, 2024, from https://www.progress.org.uk/the-ethics-of-stem-cell-research-a-hindu-view/

Bin Abdul Aziz, M. F., Morrison, M., & Kaye, J. (2018). Regulating human stem cell research and therapy in low-and middle-income countries: Malaysian perspectives. *New Genetics and Society*, *37*(1), 2–20.

Blackshaw, B. P., & Rodger, D. (2021). Why we should extend the 14-day rule. *Journal of Medical Ethics*, *47*(10), 712.

Campo-Engelstein, L., & Andaya, E. (2024). Clinicians' criteria for fetal moral status: Viability and relationality, not sentience. *Journal of Medical Ethics*, *50*(9), 634–639. https://jme.bmj.com/content/50/9/634.long

Castelyn, G. (2020). Embryo experimentation: Is there a case for moving beyond the '14-day rule'. *Monash Bioethics Review*, *38*(2), 181–196. https://link.springer.com/article/10.1007/s40592-020-00117-x

Dabu, C. (2004, June 22). Stem-cell science stirs debate in Muslim world, too. The Christian Science Monitor. https://www.csmonitor.com/2005/0622/p15s02-wogi.html

Darnovsky, M. (2018). *Genetically modifying future children isn't just wrong: It would harm all of us*. Retrieved September 22, 2024, from https://www.theguardian.com/commentisfree/2018/jul/17/genetically-modifying-future-children-embryos-nuffield-council-bioethics

Davis, J. J. (2004). *Evangelical ethics: Issues facing the Church today*. P & R Pub.

Deglincerti, A., Croft, G. F., Pietila, L. N., Zernicka-Goetz, M., Siggia, E. D., & Brivanlou, A. H. (2016). Self-organization of the in vitro attached human embryo. *Nature*, *533*(7602), 251–254. https://core.ac.uk/reader/211391654?utm_source=linkout

Dulak, J., & Pecyna, M. (2023). Unproven cell interventions in Poland and the exploitation of European Union law on advanced therapy medicinal products. *Stem Cell Reports*, *18*(8), 1610–1620.

Dyson, A., & Harris, J. (2012). *Experiments on embryos*. Routledge.

Ehrich, K., Farsides, B., Williams, C., & Scott, R. (2007). Testing the embryo, testing the fetus. *Clinical Ethics*, *2*(4), 181–186. https://pmc.ncbi.nlm.nih.gov/articles/PMC2312333/pdf/ukmss-1532w.pdf

Eich, T. (2003). Muslim voices on cloning. *ISIM Newsletter*, *12*(1), 38–39.

Foong, P. (2011). Human embryonic stem cell (HESC) research in Malaysia: Multi-faith perspectives. *Asian Bioethics Review*, *3*(3), 182–206.

Ghaly, M. (2012). The beginning of human life: Islamic bioethical perspectives. *Zygon®*, *47*(1), 175–213.

Gupta, J. A. (2012). Reproductive biocrossings: Indian egg donors and surrogates in the globalized fertility market. *International Journal of Feminist Approaches to Bioethics*, *5*(1), 25–51.

Haneef, S. S. S. (2006). *Ethics and fiqh for daily life: An Islamic outline*. International Islamic University Malaysia.
Harvey, P. (2008). A Buddhist perspective on pre-implantation genetic diagnosis. *Bionews*.
Hogan, B. (2001). From embryo to ethics: A career in science and social responsibility. An interview with Anne McLaren. *The International Journal of Developmental Biology*, *45*(3), 477–482.
Hug, K. (2006). Therapeutic perspectives of human embryonic stem cell research versus the moral status of a human embryo—Does one have to be compromised for the other. *Medicina (kaunas)*, *42*(2), 107–114.
Hurlbut, J. B., Hyun, I., Levine, A. D., Lovell-Badge, R., Lunshof, J. E., Matthews, K. R., Mills, P., Murdoch, A., Pera, M. F., & Scott, C. T. (2017). Revisiting the Warnock rule. *Nature Biotechnology*, *35*(11), 1029–1042. https://www.nature.com/articles/nbt.4015
Hyun, I., Bredenoord, A. L., Briscoe, J., Klipstein, S., & Tan, T. (2021). Human embryo research beyond the primitive streak. *Science*, *371*(6533), 998–1000.
Hyun, I., Wilkerson, A., & Johnston, J. (2016). Embryology policy: Revisit the 14-day rule. *Nature*, *533*(7602), 169–171. https://doi.org/10.1038/533169a
Ikemoto, L. C. (2009). Eggs as capital: Human egg procurement in the fertility industry and the stem cell research enterprise. *Signs*, *34*(4), 763–781.
International Society for Stem Cell Research. (2021). Guidelines for Stem Cell Research and Clinical Translation. https://www.isscr.org/guidelines
Jacxsens, L., Coveney, C., Culley, L., Lafuente-Funes, S., Pennings, G., Hudson, N., & Provoost, V. (2024). The representation of medical risks and incentives concerning egg donation: An analysis of the websites of fertility clinics of Belgium, Spain and the UK. *Human Fertility*, *27*(1), 2380667.
Jafari, M., Elahi, F., Ozyurt, S., & Wrigley, T. (2008). Religious perspectives on embryonic stem cell research. In *Fundamentals of the Stem Cell Debate:The Scientific, Religious, Ethical, and Political Issues*. Retrieved from https://escholarship.org/uc/item/9rj0k7s3
Kaczor, C. (2005). All human beings are persons. In *The edge of life: Human dignity and contemporary bioethics* (pp. 41–66). Springer.
Kaczor, C. (2022). *The ethics of abortion: Women's rights, human life, and the question of justice*. Routledge.
Kenney, N. J., & McGowan, M. L. (2014). Egg donation compensation: Ethical and legal challenges. *Medicolegal and Bioethics*, *4*, 15–24.
Keown, D. (2017). Teaching Buddhist bioethics. In *Teaching Buddhism: New insights on understanding and presenting the traditions* (pp. 296–317). Oxford University Press.
Laludin, H. (2006). Al-Maslahah (public interest) with special reference to Al-Imam Al-Ghazali. *Jurnal Syariah*, *14*(2), 103–120.
Levine, A. D. (2011). The oversight and practice of oocyte donation in the United States, United Kingdom and Canada. *HEC Forum*, *23*(1), 15–30.
Lu, M. (2011). Abortion and virtue ethics. In *Persons, moral worth, and embryos: A critical analysis of pro-choice arguments* (pp. 101–123). Springer.

Ma, H., Zhai, J., Wan, H., Jiang, X., Wang, X., Wang, L., Xiang, Y., He, X., Zhao, Z.-A., & Zhao, B. (2019). In vitro culture of cynomolgus monkey embryos beyond early gastrulation. *Science*, *366*(6467), eaax7890.

Master, Z., Matthews, K. R., & Abou-el-Enein, M. (2021). Unproven stem cell interventions: A global public health problem requiring global deliberation. *Stem Cell Reports*, *16*(6), 1435–1445.

Matthews, K. R., Iltis, A. S., Marquez, N. G., Wagner, D. S., Robert, J. S., de Melo-Martín, I., Bigg, M., Franklin, S., Holm, S., Metzler, I., Molè, M. A., Taupitz, J., Testa, G., & Sugarman, J. (2021). Rethinking human embryo research policies. *Hastings Center Report*, *51*(1), 47–51.

McCully, S. (2021). The time has come to extend the 14-day limit. *Journal of Medical Ethics*, *47*(12), e66.

McLean, A. K., Stewart, C., & Kerridge, I. (2015). Untested, unproven, and unethical: The promotion and provision of autologous stem cell therapies in Australia. *Stem Cell Research & Therapy*, *6*, 1–8.

McMahon, D. S. (2014). The global industry for unproven stem cell interventions and stem cell tourism. *Tissue Engineering and Regenerative Medicine*, *11*, 1–9.

Mohamed, Y. (1995). Fitrah and its bearing on the principles of psychology. *The American Journal of Islamic Social Sciences*, *12*(1), 1–18.

Mollaki, V. (2021). Ethical challenges in organoid use. *BioTech*, *10*(3), 12.

Nahman, M. (2011). Reverse traffic: Intersecting inequalities in human egg donation. *Reproductive Biomedicine Online*, *23*(5), 626–633.

Nordin, M. M. (2006). Islamic medical ethics amidst developing biotechnologies. In *The human genetic and reproductive technologies: Comparing religious and secular perspectives.* Islamic Organization of Medical Sciences (cited in Fadel 2010). Muslim Professionals Forum. http://mpf.org.my/wp/?p=221

Nordin, M. M. (2011). Human genetic and reproductive technologies: An international medico-legal-religious impasse? *Bangladesh Journal of Medical Science*, *10*(1), 1.

Peterson, J. C. (2003). *Is a human embryo a human being?* Georgetown University Press.

Plomer, A. (2002). Beyond the HFE Act 1990: The regulation of stem cell research in the UK. *Medical Law Review*, *10*, 132.

Promta, S. (2004). Human cloning and embryonic stem cell research. *Eubios Journal of Asian and International Bioethics*, *14*(6), 197–199.

Rahman, R. A., Sulaiman, N. A., Hashi, A. A., Rashidi, N. M., & Sha'ban, M. (2014). Bioethical issues of tissue engineering and regenerative medicine: A preliminary review from Islamic perspective. *Revelation and Science*, *4*(2).

Rajabi, M., & Khuzani, M. B. (2018). The effect of intention on the ethical value of actions from the viewpoint of the holy Qur'an. *A Biannual Journal of Ethics and Spirituality*, *8*(2).

Rispler-Chaim, V. (2006). Between Islamic law and science: Contemporary Muftis and Muslim ethicists on embryo and stem cells research. *Comparative Islamic Studies*, *2*(1).

Sagan, A., & Singer, P. (2007). The moral status of stem cells. *Metaphilosophy*, *38*(2–3), 264–284.
Schlieter, J. (2022). Buddhism and bioethics. In *Oxford research encyclopedia of religion*. Oxford University Press.
Shahbazi, M. N., Jedrusik, A., Vuoristo, S., Recher, G., Hupalowska, A., Bolton, V., Fogarty, N. M., Campbell, A., Devito, L. G., & Ilic, D. (2016). Self-organization of the human embryo in the absence of maternal tissues. *Nature Cell Biology*, *18*(6), 700–708. https://pmc.ncbi.nlm.nih.gov/articles/PMC5049689/pdf/emss-68293.pdf
Siddiqi, M. (2002). *An Islamic perpective on stem cells research*. Retrieved September 26, 2024, from http://IslamiCity.com
Singh, A. K., & McGuirk, J. P. (2016). Allogeneic stem cell transplantation: A historical and scientific overview. *Cancer Research*, *76*(22), 6445–6451.
Sipp, D. (2009). Stem cells and regenerative medicine on the Asian horizon: An economic, industry and social perspective. *Regenerative Medicine*, *4*(6), 911–918.
Sipp, D. (2011). The unregulated commercialization of stem cell treatments: A global perspective. *Frontier Medicine*, *5*, 348–355.
Sipp, D., Caulfield, T., Kaye, J., Barfoot, J., Blackburn, C., Chan, S., De Luca, M., Kent, A., McCabe, C., Munsie, M., Sleeboom-Faulkner, M., Sugarman, J., van Zimmeren, E., Zarzeczny, A., & Rasko, J. E. J. (2017). Marketing of unproven stem cell-based interventions: A call to action. *Science Translational Medicine*, *5*(9), 397.
Smith, C., Martin-Lillie, C., Higano, J. D., Turner, L., Phu, S., Arthurs, J., Nelson, T. J., Shapiro, S., & Master, Z. (2020). Challenging misinformation and engaging patients: Characterizing a regenerative medicine consult service. *Regenerative Medicine*, *15*(3), 1427–1440.
Vita, P. A. P. (2000). Declaration on the production and the scientific and therapeutic use of Human Embryonic Stem Cells. Vatican Press. http://hdl.handle.net/10822/523384
Warnock, M. (1987). Do human cells have rights? *Bioethics*, *1*(1), 1–14.

3 The governance framework in the United Kingdom, Singapore, and Malaysia

3.1 Introduction

This chapter begins by presenting an overview of the existing international regulatory instruments established to govern human stem cell research and address the ethical issues surrounding the use of human embryos for research purposes. In addition to the preceding chapter that highlights the complexities associated with determining the moral status of human embryos and the onset of life from various religious viewpoints, this chapter aims to underscore that the existing regulatory instruments do not offer clear guidance regarding the status of human embryos other than giving an emphasis to the necessity for their protection.

It then, in turn, provides an overview of the landscape of the stem cell industry and examines the existing governance framework in three selected jurisdictions namely the United Kingdom, Singapore, and Malaysia. The examination of the governance framework focuses on the establishment of laws, guidelines, and advisory bodies in addressing the identified ethical issues, as highlighted in the preceding chapter, in the respective jurisdictions.

Based on the comparison between the selected jurisdictions, this chapter demonstrates that the United Kingdom has a more established regulatory system that can be learned by other countries, particularly developing countries such as Malaysia. However, it is important to also recognise the relevance of the approach introduced by the United Kingdom, in the local context particularly the different demography, whereby Malaysia shares the similarity with Singapore than that of the United Kingdom. Therefore, Singapore also offers regulatory measures that may be more suitable for Malaysia. There are also challenges that a developing nation would face in establishing a rigorous and comprehensive regulation, which would require funding, human capital, as well as political will.

3.2 Overview of the international regulation

3.2.1 The convention of human rights and biomedicine 1997

The Convention of Human Rights and Biomedicine (CHRB) was established to protect individuals' dignity and rights in the context of biomedicine (Council

DOI: 10.4324/9781003583479-3

of Europe, 1997). It is the only international legally binding instrument on the protection of human rights in biomedical field, particularly among its State members of the Council of Europe. Its influence on the regulation of human stem cell research can be understood through several key aspects namely the principle of human dignity, informed consent, ethical oversight, moral status of human embryos, and the protection they deserve.

Principle of human dignity

The CHRB through Articles 1 and 2 emphasises the protection of human dignity, asserting that the interests and well-being of individuals must take precedence over scientific pursuits. It can be argued that this instrument provides a foundational principle that affects the ethical considerations surrounding biomedical research involving human participants such as human stem cell research and the treatment of human embryos.

Informed consent

The convention gives an emphasis to the requirement of informed consent as a tool to ensure the principle of human dignity is respected not only in medical intervention but also in scientific research. Articles 5 to 9 mandate that individuals must give voluntary, informed consent for any medical intervention and Articles 17 to 18 provide the protection for human participants undergoing research including research involving human embryos. This would ensure that participants understand the implications of their involvement in research and the potential uses of their biological materials including stem cells and embryos.

Ethical oversight

In addition to the ethical considerations in protecting the rights and dignity of human persons undergoing research, the convention under Article 16 also promotes ethical review processes for biomedical research, ensuring that research involving human persons undergoes rigorous ethical scrutiny. This enhances accountability and helps to mitigate potential risks and ethical dilemmas inherent in stem cell research.

Moral and legal status of human embryos

Nonetheless, it can be argued that the Convention does not clearly address the issue of moral and legal status of human embryos. Article 1 of CHRB reads "Parties to this Convention shall protect the dignity and identity of all human beings and guarantee everyone without discrimination, respect for their integrity and other rights and fundamental freedoms with regard to the application of biology and medicine". However, in the absence of explicit definition and explanation as to what "human beings" and "everyone" mean, the Convention invites various concepts in relation to the scientific activities involving human embryos.

Beyleveld and Brownsword (2001, p. 32) in their book stated that "the concept of 'everyone-as-a-bearer-of-human-rights' might be contested" because it might be interpreted in a way that it is only the persons who have the capacities to exercise their rights are entitled the respect and protection but excluding the non-bearer of such capacities especially the potential human beings such as embryos from protection. The question which needs a clear answer is whether "everyone" refers to all living persons as "a complete biologically well-defined human being" excluding embryo? In addition, the Convention also use other "vague and undefined terms when speaking of 'individual', 'person', 'everybody', 'human being', 'beginning of life', 'identity of human being and of human species'" (Hottois, 2000, p. 136).

While some signatories might believe that the possession and protection of human rights and dignity only recognised for actual living persons, there are other arguments stating that the protection should extend to the "*conceptus*" such as zygotes, embryos, and foetuses from the point of conception onwards (Beyleveld, 2001). The latter was supported by the Explanatory Report to the CHRB states that:

> The Convention also uses the expression 'human being' to state the necessity to protect the dignity and identity of all human beings. It was acknowledged that it was a generally accepted principle that human dignity and the identity of the human being had to be respected as soon as life began.

Notwithstanding the previous statement, one can further argue that such a provision does not help in addressing the issue of when life begins especially when the point of time that life begins is not explicitly explained, which is compounded by the fact that such a moral question is also insolvable even from the religious perspectives, as highlighted in the preceding chapter.

Protection of human embryos

It could also be argued that the Convention does not clearly recognise a human embryo as a "person" or a "human being" because it highlights the use of embryos in research under a separate provision which is under Article 18. Nevertheless, it promotes the need to offer "adequate protection" whenever research using embryos is allowed. However, the "adequate protection" is left undefined as to what kind of protection is granted. Paragraph 2 of Article 18 of the CHRB explicitly states that "the creation of human embryos for research purposes is prohibited" but there is nowhere in the Convention that prohibits research involving the destruction of human embryos.

This ambiguity would certainly lead to different interpretations and points of view which will result in non-conclusive agreement. Plomer further adds that there are a number of States which have not signed and ratified the Convention "because of deep divisions over the legitimacy of embryo research". The previous discussion shows that the Convention does not offer a clear indication as to the status of the embryo, whether it should be recognised as possessing human rights and human dignity as equivalent to "a complete biologically defined human being" and the protection granted.

3.2.2 The universal declaration on bioethics and human rights (UDBHR) 2005

The UDBHR was adopted at the international level, marking a significant advance in the pursuit of global minimum standards for biomedical research and clinical practice. This declaration addresses one of the key principles of bioethics and its relationship with human rights. The UDBHR is fundamentally rooted in the ethics and morality of scientific progress. The Preamble of the Declaration states:

> recognizing that, based on the freedom of science and research, scientific and technological developments have been, and can be, of great benefit to humankind by enhancing life expectancy and improving quality of life, and emphasizing that these developments should always aim to promote the welfare of individuals, families, groups or communities, and humankind as a whole, while acknowledging the dignity of the human person and the universal respect for, and observance of, human rights and fundamental freedoms.

The term "human dignity" appears nine times throughout the UDBHR. One of its primary objectives, as outlined in Article 2(d), is to give emphasis to the significance of the freedom and the advantages of scientific and technological advancements, whilst insisting that any research progress must adhere to the ethical principles that promote the moral obligations of researchers to respect human dignity as accentuated in the declaration. For instance, Article 2(c) states the intention of the declaration is "to promote respect for human dignity and protect human rights by ensuring respect for human life and fundamental freedoms, in accordance with international human rights law".

The UDBHR merely stated that the scope of protection granted by the declaration is applied to all human beings but as with the CHRB, the term "human beings" is not well-defined. There is nowhere in the text of the

UDBHR specifically mentioning "human embryo". Therefore, it is unclear whether the use of human embryos for research purposes is addressed by the declaration and whether human dignity is also afforded to human embryos. Some scholars note that the UDBHR introduces ambiguities regarding the interpretation of "human dignity". It was argued that Article 2(c) implies that ensuring respect for life is critical to upholding "human dignity", suggesting that the destruction of an embryo for stem cell research could indicate a lack of respect for human life, and thus, human dignity.

3.2.3 The ISSCR guidelines on stem cell research and clinical translation 2021

The International Society for Stem Cell Research (ISSCR), founded in 2002, has become the leading international organisation dedicated to all aspects of stem cell research and its clinical applications. Recognising the need for a global standard in ethical and practical research, the Society began developing guidelines early on. The first ISSCR Guidelines, published in 2006, focused primarily on human embryonic stem cells (hESCs) and recommended the establishment of stem cell research oversight committees to ensure responsible use and derivation of hESC lines. Subsequent guidelines in 2008 emphasised the clinical translation of stem cell therapies.

In 2016, the Guidelines were updated to include induced pluripotent stem cells (iPSCs) and a broader scope of human embryo research, proposing an Embryo Research Oversight (EMRO) process for comprehensive review. With significant advancements in stem cell biology, genome editing, and related clinical applications over the past five years, the ISSCR has undertaken a major revision of the Guidelines. The new 2021 Guidelines encompass various developments, including embryo culture techniques, organoid formation, chimaeras, *in vitro* gametogenesis, mitochondrial replacement, and enhanced guidance for stem cell line procurement and clinical translation (International Society for Stem Cell Research, 2021).

The updated guidelines also underscore the importance of rigorous independent review for human stem cell and embryo research while providing clearer criteria and practical guidance for oversight. This oversight process is now referred to as a "specialised scientific and ethics oversight process", capable of evaluating the unique scientific and ethical aspects of the research. The review can occur at various institutional levels and while the Guidelines do not endorse specific committees, they recommend that the review be conducted by established bodies such as Embryonic Stem Cell Research Oversight (ESCRO), Stem Cell Research Oversight (SCRO), and Embryo Research Oversight (EMRO), ESCRO, ensuring the inclusion of relevant expertise and a mix of generalists and lay members.

ISSCR three-tiered oversight system

The revised ISSCR Guidelines introduce a three-tiered system to enhance the review process for the procurement of banked and historical cell lines while ensuring a thorough evaluation for obtaining embryos and gametes for stem cell research. All procurements must adhere to established ethical research principles, including donor consent and relevant legal regulations.

TIER 1

The use of banked and historical human cell lines is allowed if they were deposited in accordance with current ethical and regulatory standards and distributed per the original consent. Importantly, these cell lines cannot be used for reproductive purposes, such as creating embryos from in vitro-derived gametes.

TIER 2

The procurement of fresh human somatic cells and tissues for stem cell research requires review by existing oversight committees, supplemented by expertise in stem cell research.

TIER 3

The procurement of human gametes and embryos intended for use in research must undergo a specialised oversight process detailed in the Guidelines. This includes monitoring donor recruitment practices to ensure that women donating oocytes or embryos are not subjected to undue inducement or exploitation.

Protection of donors

The Guidelines also emphasise the importance of protecting vulnerable individuals and populations from exploitation and stress that there should be no unacceptable influences in the provision of human cells and tissues. Additionally, donors should have the option to receive incidental findings, such as genetic risks, which must be clearly stated in the consent process. The provenance of stem cell lines should be verifiable through relevant documentation, including material transfer agreements and data that confirm the cell line's identity and permissible uses under the original consent. However, considering advances in genomic sequencing, researchers are encouraged to maintain confidentiality when sharing genomic data that could potentially identify donors or their families.

ADDRESSING PREMATURE COMMERCIALISATION OF UNPROVEN THERAPIES

The Society also recognises the increase in clinical trials as well as a rise in inappropriate interventions and misleading claims involving stem cells. To address these issues, the revised guidelines provide improved recommendations for clinical translation. For instance, the Guidelines recognise legitimate treatments involving stem cells which are being practised by genuine medical practitioners that can help those who desperately need an intervention despite the lack of evidence of its effectiveness through the standard clinical trials by endorsing accelerated approval pathways. Nonetheless, this approach is subject to a robust post-market surveillance with conditional approval.

The Guidelines also address the issue of premature commercialisation of unproven cell therapies. The instrument advocates against any clinical translation that is not aligned with international standards. For instance, it recommends the application of internationally accepted regulatory measures such as the classification of stem cell products as drugs or advanced therapy medicinal products (ATMPs) when they are substantially manipulated or used for non-homologous purposes. This measure is consistent with regulations adopted by various regulatory bodies across the globe such as the US Food and Drug Administration (FDA), European Medicines Agency (EMA), and Australia's Therapeutic Goods Administration (TGA). The Guidelines also recommend the establishment of patient registries with the aim to keep track of disease histories and long-term outcomes instead of being utilised as substitutes for randomised controlled trials that are needed for product marketing authorisation as well as advertising tools that can mislead patients.

3.3 Overview of the United Kingdom's governance framework

3.3.1 The landscape of stem cell industry

The United Kingdom is home to several distinguished research institutions specialising in stem cell biology. Notably, The Wellcome Trust-MRC Cambridge Stem Cell Institute stands at the forefront of pluripotent stem cell research, bringing together 30 leading research teams with expertise in the use of three main types of stem cells namely embryonic, adult, and pluripotent stem cells to research on developmental biology, disease modelling, and regenerative medicine. The Oxford Stem Cell Institute, which comprises 40 laboratories across Oxford, engages in pioneering research on development biology as well as stem cell therapies for conditions such as Parkinson's disease, diabetes, and cancer. Additionally, the Stem Cell and Regenerative Medicine Research Centre at King's College London focuses on translating stem cell discoveries into clinical applications, particularly in developing cellular therapies for cardiovascular disease. The centre initiated "Stem Cell Hotel" to provide dedicated laboratory space for collaborative studies. The groundbreaking induced pluripotent stem cells (iPSCs) technology is extensively employed for disease modelling, drug testing, and personalised medicine in the United Kingdom. Furthermore, UK researchers are utilising CRISPR technology to edit genes within stem cells, facilitating the investigation of genetic disorders and the potential development of therapies aimed at correcting genetic mutations.

Clinical translation efforts

The United Kingdom has initiated numerous clinical trials designed to evaluate the efficacy and safety of stem cell-based therapies. For instance, ongoing trials are investigating the use of stem cells to treat conditions such as Parkinson's disease, osteoarthritis, Huntington's disease, multiple sclerosis, corneal blindness, and advanced cancer. Researchers are also examining the potential of cardiac stem cell therapies to restore heart tissue following myocardial infarction, with the goal of demonstrating improvements in cardiac function and patient outcomes. Additionally, numerous trials are focused on utilising hematopoietic stem cells to address various haematological disorders, including leukaemia and lymphoma. These initiatives receive strong backing from the UK's National Health Service (NHS), which emphasises their critical role in addressing severe medical conditions.

Industry and collaborative efforts

The UK stem cell industry is characterised by collaborative endeavours among academia, industry, and government entities (Curle et al., 2024). Numerous biotechnology startups are concentrated on stem cell technologies, striving to develop commercial applications for regenerative medicine. Initiatives like the UK Stem Cell Hub facilitate collaboration between research institutions and private enterprises, thereby enhancing innovation and expediting the translation of scientific discoveries into clinical practice. Moreover, the UK government, alongside organisations such as the Wellcome Trust, the Medical Research Council (MRC), and a few other agencies, have made substantial investments in stem cell research, providing grants to support both basic and applied research initiatives. For instance, the MRC together with the Biotechnology and Biological Sciences Research Council, and Engineering and Physical Sciences Research Council established the UK Regenerative Medicine Platform as a collaborative approach to target the translational challenges of regenerative medicine, whereby they also establish interdisciplinary research hubs that unite expertise in stem cell biology and regenerative medicine to address the knowledge gap to accelerate applications. Translational effort in the United Kingdom is also supported by companies such as ReNeuron and Celltech Pharma is at the forefront of pioneering stem cell therapies with the potential for significant market impact.

3.3.2 Advisory body

The United Kingdom does not possess a singular advisory body, or a national bioethics committee dedicated to addressing bioethical concerns. Instead, a multitude of organisations and committees, such as the Human Genetics Commission, collaborate to provide counsel to pertinent stakeholders, including the government, scientists, and the public, on bioethical issues arising from various domains of science and medicine. Among these entities, the Nuffield Council on Bioethics has been notably proactive in engaging with bioethical dilemmas within the United Kingdom. Established in 1991 by the Nuffield Foundation, a private charitable trust, the Council has received funding from the Medical Research Council and the Wellcome Trust since 1994. The Nuffield Council asserts that it is the only organisation in the United Kingdom with a comprehensive bioethics horizon scanning program. This approach facilitates the identification and anticipation of future developments in biomedicine and health that may impact society. Such a methodology allows the Council to refine its programmatic focus and influence policy agendas effectively. The Council's primary responsibilities include: (i) identifying and articulating ethical questions stemming from advancements in biological and medical research, (ii) examining and reporting on these questions to enhance public understanding, thereby potentially leading to the formulation of new guidelines by relevant authorities, and (iii) publishing reports and making appropriate representations.

The Council has produced an extensive array of reports and discussion papers addressing a wide range of bioethical issues. The presidency of the Council is appointed by the Nuffield Foundation in consultation with other funding bodies. In contrast, the remaining members of the Council are appointed independently, with recruitment conducted through public announcements, including advertisements in the national press, newsletters, and the Council's website. Currently, the Council comprises 15 members, all of whom are skilled professionals from diverse fields such as philosophy, medicine, law, bioethics, policy, public affairs, and science. They serve three-year terms, with the possibility of a subsequent three-year extension. Notably, although the Council receives funding from external organisations, it operates independently and is regarded as a non-partisan entity.

When addressing pertinent topics, the Council identifies an area requiring exploration and establishes a Working Party to investigate and report on the associated issues. Topics previously examined by the Council include "egg freezing", "genome editing and human reproduction", "xenotransplantation", "embryo and stem cell research", and "artificial intelligence". A typical

Working Party consists of 10 to 18 experts from relevant disciplines, including two members of the Council and potentially lay members. The Working Party's deliberations generally involve stakeholder meetings, site visits to relevant organisations, and public consultations. The subsequent report is produced in consultation with the Council, which also coordinates dissemination activities to share findings not only with influential stakeholders but also with the public and dedicated educational subgroups. As a non-statutory body, the Council's recommendations are not legally binding, and policymakers are under no obligation to accept them. Nevertheless, the Council has established a track record that demonstrates its influence in shaping policy-making processes and legal decisions. For example, the European Court of Human Rights endorsed the Council's recommendations against the storage of DNA profiles and samples from innocent individuals on the UK's National DNA Database, ruling unanimously that retaining samples and fingerprints from two UK men who had been arrested but not convicted constituted a violation of their human rights.

Recommendations on the use of human embryos

The Council has made significant contributions to addressing bioethical dilemmas surrounding the use of human embryos for research purposes, having published two reports on this subject. In 2000, the Council's report examined the ethical implications of utilising stem cells derived from donated embryos, embryos specifically created for research, cadaveric foetal tissue, and somatic cell nuclear transfer (SCNT) (Nuffield Council on Bioethics, 2000). The report concluded that cultivating cells from a donated embryo does not signify a lack of respect for the human embryo. Furthermore, the Council contended that there are no valid moral distinctions between research into reproduction or diagnostic methods and research into potential therapies, thereby recommending that research involving human embryos be permitted for the purpose of developing tissues to treat diseases derived from embryonic stem cells. It proposed incorporating this permission into Schedule 2 of the Human Fertilisation and Embryology Act (1990). The Council also differentiated between therapeutic and reproductive cloning, asserting that the latter is explicitly prohibited under UK law while research into SCNT may yield significant medical benefits through the production of stem cells suitable for cell and tissue therapies. It recommends that as long as such research falls within the ambit of the Human Fertilisation and Embryology Act, it should be permissible to obtain a licence under Schedule 2. Additionally, the Council acknowledged that issues of consent involving the use of embryonic tissue for research present distinct challenges compared to other forms of research permissible under Schedule 2. Consequently, it recommended that embryo donors be explicitly asked whether they consent to such research and the subsequent utilisation of the cell line.

Revisiting the time limits on maintaining human embryos for research

In 2016, the Council revisited the contentious issue of human embryos used for research, focusing on the necessity of altering or maintaining the 14-day statutory limit for the culture of live human embryos (Nuffield Council on Bioethics, 2017). Many participants concurred that, while the 14-day rule may appear arbitrary, it is essential for providing a concrete framework given the complexities surrounding the moral status and values associated with human embryos. Although it remains uncertain whether this rule can reconcile the various ethical values associated with embryos, there was a consensus that its introduction as a policy tool has facilitated scientific progress while ensuring public confidence in both the research and regulatory systems. Furthermore, due to its legislative status, the 14-day rule is perceived as crucial in securing public acceptability, especially in garnering support from those who may be ambivalent about the use of human embryos for research, as it provides assurance that such research will be appropriately regulated.

The potential scientific opportunities arising from an extension of the time limit were also discussed, with suggested benefits including advances in regenerative medicine, enhanced understanding of epigenetics, and insights into cellular signalling and fate determination, all of which could lead to various clinical therapies. While some argued that scientists should fulfil the promises of research within the current temporal constraints, others contended that the demand for complete understanding up to 14 days is incongruent with the scientific method and that increasing knowledge itself should be regarded as a positive outcome. The Council also considered a possible "twin track" regulatory approach, wherein the 14-day rule would apply to interventional activities while being relaxed or extended for observational research endeavours. Nevertheless, the implications of any changes to the 14-day rule on public perception remain uncertain. It is noteworthy that the Council did not propose a specific course of action in response to this question but rather highlighted that the potential scientific benefits associated with extending the time limit could not yet be definitively established, at least within the UK context.

3.3.3 Laws

The Human Fertilisation and Embryology Act 1990

In 1978, British scientists significantly advanced the field of reproductive medicine by successfully introducing the world's first "test-tube baby" (Kuo, 1996). This groundbreaking achievement, however, precipitated a series of ethical controversies, leading to the establishment of the Committee of Inquiry into Human Fertilisation and Embryology, referred to hereafter as the Warnock Committee, under the leadership of Warnock (1985). The Committee comprised experts from various disciplines, including medical practitioners, social workers, legal scholars, and ethicists.

Although the Warnock Report was published in 1984, it took six years for the government to enact corresponding legislation. Most of the recommendations presented in the Report were accepted by the government of the time and were given legal effect through the enactment of the Human Fertilisation and Embryology Act in 1990 (hereafter, the HFE Act 1990, Human Fertilisation and Embryology Act, 1990). This Act was established to regulate the use of human embryos, primarily for reproductive purposes and secondarily for research. It is noteworthy that prior to the introduction of the HFE Act 1990, the Unborn Children (Protection) Bill was proposed in 1985, one year after the publication of the Warnock Report. The Bill garnered significant support, with the majority of Members of Parliament (MPs) voting in favour, while a minority opposed it (Jackson, 2006). Had it been enacted, the Bill would have imposed additional restrictions on abortion, expanded the rights of the embryo, and potentially altered its legal status and rights, thereby imposing severe restrictions on human embryonic research. However, the Bill failed to pass and was subsequently followed by the introduction of the Human Fertilisation and Embryology Bill in 1989, following a government consultation paper and white paper, which were successfully enacted the following year.

The Warnock Committee recommended that human embryos should be afforded some protection in law concerning the use of human embryos for research; however, this protection should not be absolute. The Committee suggested that embryo research be permitted only up to 14 days post-fertilisation, coinciding with the appearance of the primitive streak. This recommendation represented a moral compromise and a pragmatic approach to a contentious moral issue. Furthermore, the Committee advised that such research should be conducted exclusively under a licenced framework, asserting that it would constitute a criminal offence to conduct research beyond the established statutory time limit. These recommendations were incorporated into the Human Fertilisation and Embryology Act of 1990 (HFE Act, 1990), which also authorised the creation of human embryos for research purposes. The HFE Act 1990 instituted penalties of up to ten years of imprisonment for violations of its statutory requirements. Additionally, the Committee proposed the establishment of a regulatory body empowered to grant licences for human embryonic research and in-vitro fertilisation (IVF) treatments. The UK Parliament endorsed the recommendations made by the Warnock Committee, leading to the establishment of the Human Fertilisation and Embryology Authority (hereafter, the HFEA) under the Human Fertilisation and Embryology Act of 1990 (HFE Act, 1990). This Act vested the HFEA with licencing authority and assigned it the responsibility of overseeing human embryonic research. Section 3 of the HFE Act 1990 prohibits the creation and use of human embryos without obtaining a licence. Additionally, Schedule 8 of the HFE Act 1990 delineates the functions of the HFEA. The Committee emphasised the critical importance of informed consent from donors for the use of surplus embryos created through *in vitro* fertilisation (IVF) for research purposes. This emphasis on consent is mirrored in the HFE Act 1990, which includes specific provisions detailing the requirements regarding embryos utilised for research. Initially, the HFE Act 1990 permitted research on human embryos only in specific circumstances and for five distinct purposes, primarily related to congenital diseases and infertility treatment. These purposes were subsequently expanded through the Regulations of 2001 and the revised HFE Act in 2008.

The HFE Act 1990 was initially introduced without the foresight of the emerging scientific advances relating to the derivation of human embryonic stem cell (hESC) lines. In 1997, Dr. James Thomson and his team became the first scientists to successfully derive and maintain hESCs in a culture. This development raised concerns in the United Kingdom regarding whether hESC research clearly fell within the scope of the permitted purposes outlined in Schedule 2, Paragraph 3(2) of the HFE Act 1990 (Morgan, 2007). Subsequent to a series of consultations and parliamentary debates in 2000, the list of permitted purposes in Schedule 2, Paragraph 3(3) of the HFE Act 1990 was amended to include "projects of research which increase knowledge about the creation and development of embryos, or about disease, or enable such knowledge to be applied (Morgan, 2007)". As has been argued by scientists, hESC research is instrumental in furthering our understanding of embryonic development and in the treatment of various diseases within the human body. Therefore, if Schedule 2, Paragraph 3(3) is interpreted broadly, it effectively positions the HFE Act 1990 as the governing legislation for hESC research. Although the HFE Act 1990 was not explicitly designed to regulate hESC research, its application to such research is inferred due to the necessity of using *in vitro* human embryos to derive stem cells. Consequently, hESC research falls within the jurisdiction of the HFE Act 1990 and the HFEA.

The creation of human embryos *in vitro* for research purposes has been regulated and permitted since the enactment of the HFE Act 1990. However, it was not until the development of the Cell Nuclear Replacement technique for creating human embryos, which is essentially a cloning technique that questions arose concerning the scope of application of the HFE Act 1990. This issue is addressed in further detail in the following discussion.

The Human Fertilisation and Embryology (Research Purposes) Regulations 2001

The influential paper by Wilmut on cloning was published to announce a significant advancement in stem cell research, specifically through a cloning technique known as cell nuclear replacement (CNR), which facilitated the creation of Dolly, the first cloned sheep, in 1997 (Wilmut et al., 1997). The CNR method entails the removal of the nucleus from a somatic cell (in

Dolly's case, a cell from the mammary gland) and the subsequent fusion of this nucleus with an enucleated oocyte. This breakthrough opened new avenues for employing CNR to create embryos intended for research in therapeutic contexts—often referred to as therapeutic cloning. Such an approach holds the potential to produce human organs and tissues that could be transplanted into recipients without the risk of immune rejection, as the embryos created would be genetically identical to the respective donors.

However, this technique also raised ethical concerns regarding its possible use for reproductive cloning, particularly the cloning of humans. In response to these developments, the Human Fertilisation and Embryology Authority (HFEA) and the Human Genetics Advisory Commission (HGAC) collaborated to conduct public consultations aimed at gauging societal perspectives on the acceptability of therapeutic cloning and the utilisation of CNR for such purposes. The subsequent review concluded that therapeutic cloning was acceptable, leading to an extension of the research purposes permissible under the Human Fertilisation and Embryology Act 1990 (HFE Act), thereby ensuring that therapeutic cloning fell within the ambit of the Act.

In 2001, new regulations, specifically the Human Fertilisation and Embryology (Research Purposes) Regulations 2001 (hereafter referred to as the HFE Regulations 2001), were instituted to permit the licencing of cell nuclear replacement for therapeutic cloning by the HFEA. The scope of permitted research purposes was broadened to include enhancing the understanding of embryos and serious diseases as well as applying this knowledge in the development of treatments. Neither the HFEA nor the Government anticipated the legal complexities that would arise regarding the definition and scope of the term "embryo", as highlighted in the Quintavelle litigation, whereby the applicant, Bruno Quintavelle claimed that the definition of "embryo" in the HFE Act 1990 does not include embryos created by CNR and argued that s.1(1)(a) of the HFE Act 1990 only applied to embryos which created by fertilisation ("*R* (on the application of Quintavalle) *v Secretary of State for Health*"; "*Regina v Secretary of State for Health* (Respondent) ex parte Quintavalle (on behalf of Pro-Life Alliance) (Appellant)").

This legal issue pertained to whether an embryo produced via the CNR method constitutes an embryo as defined under the statutory framework of the HFE Act 1990. This matter was litigated by the UK Pro-Life Alliance and brought before both the High Court and the Court of Appeal. Justice Crane of the High Court ruled in favour of the applicant; however, this decision was subsequently overturned by the Court of Appeal. The Court justified that embryos created through CNR are fundamentally equivalent to those formed by fertilisation, as both types can develop into viable organisms of their respective species. The Court of Appeal's ruling was upheld by the House of Lords, where the Law Lords—most notably Lord Bingham, Lord Steyn, and Lord Miller-strongly dismissed the claims posited by Quintavelle.

A significant consideration for the Law Lords was the concern that embryos generated through CNR would remain unregulated if excluded from the provisions of the HFE 1990 Act, which contradicted the legislative intent at the time of the Act's enactment. In 2004, the HFEA issued the first licence for therapeutic cloning research. The UK government further solidified its commitment to human embryonic stem cell (hESC) research by establishing the UK Stem Cell Initiative (UKSCI) in 2005, with the aim of ensuring that the United Kingdom retains its status as a global leader in stem cell research and maintains its competitive advantage in this critical area of scientific inquiry.

Human-admixed embryo and the Human Fertilisation and Embryology Act 2008

Much has evolved since 1990, as stem cell research has made considerable strides, enabling scientists to create not only traditional embryos but also interspecies embryos, commonly referred to as "human admixed embryos" or animal-human hybrid embryos. In a 2000 report prepared by Sir Liam Donaldson's expert group, he explicitly opposed this development, asserting that the "mixing of human adult somatic cells with the live eggs of any animal species should not be permitted" (Chief Medical Officer's Expert Group Reviewing the Potential of Developments on Stem Cell Research and Cell Nuclear Replacement to Benefit Human Health, 2000). In August 2005, the Science Media Centre provided a platform for scientists to inform both the public and policymakers about the potential applications of hybrid embryos. This discussion culminated in a significant milestone in November 2006 when researchers from King's College London and Newcastle University submitted applications to create stem cells derived from hybrid embryos for research purposes. Although the government initially proposed prohibiting this practice, a concurrent white paper suggested enacting new legislation to include provisions permitting the regulated creation of hybrid and chimera embryos *in vitro* for research purposes.

To evaluate the permissibility of this research and to gather public opinion, the Human Fertilisation and Embryology Authority (HFEA) conducted a public consultation on "Hybrids and Chimeras" in April 2007. Following this consultation, a draft Human Fertilisation and Embryology Bill was published, explicitly allowing certain categories of interspecies embryos. Both the Human Genetics Commission and the Commons Select Committee expressed their support for hybrid embryo research, leading to its eventual sanctioning under the HFE Act 2008. Subsequent to a review and amendment of the HFE Act 1990, the new legislation namely, the Human Fertilisation and Embryology Act 2008 (hereafter referred to as the HFE Act 2008), was introduced ("Human Fertilisation and Embryology Act", 2008). The HFE Act 2008 not only sanctioned research involving human admixed embryos but also authorised the issuance of licences for their creation in vitro, provided that such research served permitted purposes.[1] In 2008, the HFEA announced the approval of two research projects utilising human-animal hybrid embryos. The decision to permit hybrid embryo research, contingent upon adherence to HFEA restrictions, underscores the argument that the United Kingdom's regulatory approach is both tightly controlled and permissive.

Significant changes were made to the provisions governing human embryonic research, broadening the scope of permitted research purposes outlined in the HFE Act 2008 compared to the HFE Act 1990. Notably, Schedule 2, Paragraph 3A(2)(b) of the HFE Act 2008 allows for research aimed at increasing knowledge about "serious diseases" as well as "other serious medical conditions", thus expanding the focus beyond the previous terminology of "serious disease" found in the 2001 Regulations, which did not accommodate the study of injuries not categorised as diseases. The 2001 Regulations were subsequently repealed and replaced by the HFE Act 2008. The term "serious disease" in the earlier Regulations had a more restrictive connotation while the broader phrase "medical conditions" in the 2008 Act potentially encompasses a wider range of research topics, including injuries. As Pattinson notes, "[i]t is now clearer that the legislation authorises (1) basic research and (2) research into serious injuries not amounting to a disease, such as spinal cord injuries", aligning with the United Kingdom's controlled yet permissive approach (Pattison, 2009). The new Act, while extending the permitted research purposes, maintains a requirement for conduct within a controlled environment subject to specific regulations.

In her analysis, Rossi concurs, viewing the HFE Act 2008 as more permissive due to its comprehensive language, which avoids narrowing the scope of research (Rossi, 2009). This legislative framework does not hinder the government's efforts to foster advancements in this scientific domain and to ensure that the United Kingdom remains a leader in this area of science. Furthermore, as the HFE Act governs the use and storage of human admixed embryos, provisions concerning consent have also been expanded to include these embryos. Specifically, the Act introduces a provision requiring explicit consent for the use and storage of human admixed embryos.

Additionally, the HFE Act 2008 mandates that consent must be documented in writing and signed by the individual providing it. This stringent requirement underscores the controlled permissive approach adopted by the United Kingdom. While the United Kingdom is dedicated to promoting human embryonic research, it is equally committed to safeguarding the rights of donors by emphasising the importance of consent in its legislation, thereby minimising potential misconduct related to disregard or misuse of consent. Once again, the UK government has established a "progressive and well-developed embryonic research licencing and regulatory regime (Belew, 2003)".

1 Human Fertilisation and Embryology Act 2008, Schedule 2 Paragraph 6(3)(3) (2008).

3.3.4 Guidelines

It is important to note that both the Human Fertilisation and Embryology Act 1990 (HFE Act, 1990) and the Human Fertilisation and Embryology Act 2008 (HFE Act, 2008) specifically regulate research involving the use of human embryos for the derivation of human embryonic stem cell lines. Neither Act addresses research that utilises already established human embryonic stem cell lines. This regulatory gap was highlighted in the 2002 Report of the House of Lords Select Committee. The Wellcome Trust noted in its evidence that no current legislation governs the distribution or research involving stem cell lines once they have been derived from embryos. Despite the opportunity presented by the revision of the HFE Act to close this gap, it was concluded that established stem cell lines do not qualify as embryos and hence do not require the same level of regulatory oversight.

However, the use of established embryonic stem cell lines is not left entirely unregulated. Any research that involves the derivation of human embryonic stem cell lines must adhere to the procedures and conditions set forth by the HFEA's licencing requirements. Licencees are mandated to deposit each derived stem cell line in the UK Stem Cell Bank, which serves as a repository for human embryonic stem cell lines and other types of cell lines. This repository ensures the availability of ethically sourced and quality-controlled human stem cell lines at a centralised location. In addition to storing these cell lines, the UK Stem Cell Bank plays a crucial role in regulating their use. Individuals seeking to obtain stem cell lines deposited after April 2010 must sign a research use licence that stipulates the terms of use for the requested cell lines. Any secondary research or the transfer of these stem cell lines to third parties is prohibited without the explicit approval of the UK Stem Cell Bank Steering Committee (hereinafter referred to as the Steering Committee). The Steering Committee is tasked with developing and monitoring the implementation of a code of practice that governs the Bank and the use of stem cell lines. Thus, the regulatory responsibility initially held by the HFEA is transferred to the Steering Committee in instances where research does not involve human embryos but utilises established stem cells or stem cell lines.

In 2010, the Steering Committee produced a code of practice for stem cell lines to provide guidance on the utilisation of stem cell lines and to outline supervisory mechanisms for research involving human embryonic stem cell lines. This code is specifically limited to established stem cell lines derived from human embryos, which necessitate the destruction of those embryos (UK Stem Cell Bank Steering Committee, 2010). Consequently, other pluripotent stem cell lines fall outside the purview of this code, as its primary aim is to ensure that research on human embryonic stem cell lines is conducted within an ethical framework. Given that these cell lines contain the genetic information of the individual from whom they were derived, the Steering Committee retains the authority to oversee research involving any embryonic stem cell lines, regardless of their source, whether from the UK Stem Cell Bank or elsewhere. Additionally, any activities related to the import and export of stem cell lines or the acquisition of lines from external sources must be submitted for approval to the Steering Committee.

In contrast to the HFEA, which requires that research proposals receive prior approval from a Research Ethics Committee (REC) before submitting a licence application, the Steering Committee does not necessitate REC approval for research involving embryonic stem cell lines if the research is solely for basic laboratory purposes. Nevertheless, the Steering Committee, similar to the HFEA licencing committee, has established its own application procedures and requirements that must be fulfilled prior to granting approval for the use of embryonic stem cell lines. The Code of Practice delineates a list of permitted research purposes aligned with those specified in the HFE Act 1990 and amended by the HFE Act 2008. Consequently, the moral compromises surrounding human embryonic research have resulted in a permissive yet controlled regulatory environment, facilitated by the adoption of the HFE Act and its subsequent adaptations pertaining to stem cell research.

3.4 Overview of Singapore's governance framework

3.4.1 The landscape of stem cell industry

As has been widely reported, Ariff Bongso, a Singaporean scientist and his research group were the first to derive human embryonic stem cells (hESCs) from a 5-day-old human blastocyst in 1994 (Bongso et al., 1994). The discovery took place at the National University of Singapore. Then, another success story in stem cell research was reported in 1998 whereby James Thomson and his team at the University of Wisconsin produced long-lived hESC cultures (Thomson et al., 1998). Both discoveries have led to an excitement among the research community and high hopes among the public worldwide of its potential application in regenerative medicine. Since then, stem cell research has been recognised by the Singaporean Government as the way forward in regenerative medicine and categorised as one of the prioritised R&D initiatives in the country.

Collaboration and capital mass

Not only that, as has been mentioned by Alan Colman,

> Singapore plans to become a provider of new human embryonic and adult stem cell lines and of reagents for drug discovery and drug testing, an objective facilitated by the new A*STAR Experimental Therapeutics Centre . . . led by British cancer researcher David Lane.
>
> (Colman, 2008)

It can be said that the discovery by Ariff had a significant impact on the government's recognition towards this area, which led to the establishment of its first stem cell start-up company known as ES Cell International Pte Ltd (ESI) in 2000. Since then, there has been an increase in the number of talents in various stem cell research works at universities, hospitals, and research institutes. Furthermore, a dedicated body has been established, the A*STAR Singapore Stem Cell Consortium to give support to the research community. The consortium reportedly administers approximately US$ 75 million of government funding for intramural and extramural stem cell research over five years.

In doing so, it has been reported that the government has approximately invested more than US$ 4 billion in establishing a modern and strong centralised and integrated scientific and clinical infrastructure (Colman, 2008). There is a dedicated government agency, Agency for Science Technology and Research (A*STAR) established in 2000, and the agency itself has established 14 research institutions. Many of these institutions are in the Biopolis complex, which was reported to cost more than US$ 400 million when it was opened in 2003.

Singapore has demonstrated that collaboration between local and foreign talents is key to developing this potential area. It can be seen from the involvement of foreign talents in developing this area in Singapore, notably, in establishing Biopolis and A*STAR Experimental Therapeutics Centre. Nevertheless, Singapore also realised the importance of building its own local talents. When A*STAR was established, the training of upcoming generations of home-grown scientists was a key aspect of the Government's vision for economic development. This initiative encompassed both public sector research facilities and privately funded research projects, such as those at the Temasek Life Sciences Institute. It was targeted that by 2015, A*STAR would have trained an additional 1,000 Singaporean scientists at the PhD level, with education both locally and at select institutions overseas.

Advancing stem cell research and therapy in Singapore

Singapore aspires to develop and manufacture stem cell-based therapies to achieve its goal to be the centre of this modern treatment in the world (Colman, 2008). Stem cell research and treatment in Singapore are indeed progressing rapidly. Stem cell treatments have been conducted as early as 2004, whereby limbal stem cells and autologous transplants of cultivated human conjunctival stem cell explants are used to treat a variety of ocular surface injuries. Later in 2010, it was reported that the Singapore Stem Cell Bank had generated human embryonic stem cell banks from clinical-grade cell lines to facilitate the translation of human embryonic stem cells-based research to clinical trials (Sivarajah et al., 2010). In April 2023, it was reported scientists at Duke-NUS Medical School, the Singapore Eye Research Institute, and the Karolinska Institute in Sweden reported a successful preclinical study using stem cells to produce progenitor photoreceptor cells in restoring retinal function (Tay et al., 2023). In 2020, the Advanced Cell Therapy and Research Institute, Singapore (ACTRIS) was established to facilitate the advancement of cellular-based treatment in Singapore the meet the increasing demand for such therapies. In June 2023, it was reported that a stem cell-based therapy for heart failure developed by the Duke-NUS Medical School researchers showed promising results in preclinical trials (Yap et al., 2023). Recently in July 2024, researchers from the National University of Singapore's Yong Loo Lin School of Medicine announced the promising potential stem cell-based gene therapy for glioblastoma (brain tumour) patients by late 2025.

3.4.2 Advisory body

The Singaporean Cabinet in December 2000 established the Bioethics Advisory Committee (BAS) with the mandate to examine the ethical, legal, and social issues arising from biomedical sciences research in Singapore. The Committee is comprised of experts from different backgrounds such as medicine, law, and sociologist, including religious scholars. The Committee plays a role as a policy advisory body and has no regulatory power. It does not address issues involving the use of animals for research but if the research involves the combination of human and animal tissues or affects the welfare of human subjects, then it falls within the ambit of the Committee. In carrying out its role, the Committee is guided by the three thrusts: (i) protection of the rights and welfare of individuals; (ii) public education and a source of information on bioethical issues; and (iii) identify broad principles to govern the ethical, legal, and social implications of human biology research. The Committee is also actively engaging with their counterparts internationally through various activities including conferences and visits to foreign centres. So far, the Committee has published 12 consultation papers and 11 reports on various biomedical issues such as genetic testing, human tissue research, and neuroscience research. The earliest report and consultation paper that the Committee has produced are on human stem cell research and reproductive and therapeutic cloning.

Under its purview, the BAC has established the Human Stem Cell Research Subcommittee to address the ethical, legal and social issues arising specifically from human stem cell research, including the issues of human therapeutic and reproductive cloning. In its effort to address this contentious issue, the BAC conducted a thorough public consultation to obtain opinions and views from the Singaporean community. It also conducted dialogue sessions with various groups including those representing religious, patient, professional, research and medical dimensions as well as welcomed their views in written submissions and even letters from the public.

After its establishment, Singapore's Bioethics Advisory Committee (BAC) put forward recommendations to the Ministerial Committee for Life Sciences, for Singapore policies to govern stem cell research. After its public consultation, the BAC in its report recommended that (i) research on human adult stem cells is ethically acceptable; (ii) use of cadaveric foetal tissues is allowed provided there is informed consent and ethical abortion; (iii) use of surplus embryos is allowed for research subject to the 14-day rule; (iv) in case of limitations where there are no alternatives, creation of human embryos is on a case-by-case basis and with specific statutory approval from a regulatory body; and (v) reproductive cloning by any method is strictly banned (Committee, 2002).

Furthermore, the BAC recommended that the UK regulatory system be used as a basic model. However, necessary modifications and refinements should be made as deemed necessary. The most significant modification that the Committee has pointed out is to have a more inclusive regulatory framework. Instead of having a statutory body that only governs the use of human embryos for research, the BAC further recommends that a statutory body be established and should be vested in a board to licence, audit, control, and monitor all human stem cell research.

In addition, licences granted by the statutory body should be all-encompassing, that is, to incorporate the derivation, storage, and use of research materials—a more inclusive approach. It is also recommended that the statutory body be vested a legal power to impose sanctions including criminal penalties in the case of non-compliance with the regulation and law.

3.4.3 Laws

At this point of writing, Singapore has no comprehensive legal framework that specifically governs the use of human embryos for research compared to its counterparts such as the United Kingdom. The existing Directives for Private Healthcare Institutions providing assisted reproduction services do not primarily govern human embryo research. They only provide permission for the secondary use of IVF-created human embryos that are not used for fertility treatment, provided regulation requirements are met such as the 14-day rule.

The establishment of a legal framework

The Singapore Cabinet accepted all the BAC's recommendations and followed up by passing of Regulation of Biomedical Research Bill in November 2003. Instead of enacting a piece of legislation specifically to regulate human stem cell research, after the recommendations, the government decided to take a step-by-step approach. A bigger issue at stake, human cloning, was addressed first by enacting the Human Cloning and Other Prohibited Practices Act 2004 (hereafter, the Human Cloning Act 2004) (Human Cloning and Other Prohibited Practices Act, 2004 (Singapore)). When this Act 2004 was enacted, the government decided that there would be separate laws to govern human embryonic stem cell research and human tissue research.

Some of the key provisions of the Human Cloning Act 2004 are: (i) Section 5 prohibits the implantation of a human embryo clone in the body of a human or an animal; (ii) therapeutic cloning of human embryos for research is allowed under special circumstances; (iii) Section 7 bans the implantation of any human embryo created by any other method than fertilisation of egg and sperm for longer than fourteen days; (iv) bans import and export of human embryo clones; (v) prohibits commercial trading in human eggs, human sperm and human embryos; and (vi) imposes criminal penalties for contravening the Human Cloning and Other Prohibited Practices Act.

Singapore's approach is fundamentally based on the concepts of beneficence and non-malfeasance. The government believes that beneficial research should be carried out, but the risks from the research should be weighed against the expected benefits. Since there is no clear-cut evidence of which source of stem cells is the best for developing treatment and given that different stem cell sources have different disadvantages and advantages, it would be better to continue to use all sources of stem cells in ethically acceptable research to resolve the puzzle.

In 2015, the Singapore Government established the Human Biomedical Research Act to govern all forms of biomedical research including human stem cell research, which later was revised in 2020 (Human Biomedical Research Act, 2015). Nonetheless, stem cell research involving human gametes and embryos including human-animal combinations is subject to a more stringent regulatory control, which also falls under the Human Biomedical Research (Restricted Research) Regulations 2017 (Human Biomedical Research (Restricted Research) Regulations, 2017). Any research involving the use of cell, tissue, and gene therapy products is governed by the Health Products (Clinical Trials) Regulations 2016 (Health Products (Clinical Trials) Regulations, 2016) as mandated under Section 72 of the Health Products Act 2007 (Health Products Act, 2007).

The Human Biomedical Research Act 2015 establishes essential regulations governing research involving human embryos, human gametes, and human stem cells, distinguishing between prohibited and restricted practices. The Third Schedule outlines prohibited research, which includes the development of human-animal combination embryos for more than 14 days or past the appearance of the primitive streak—whichever comes first—as well as the implantation of such embryos into either humans or animals. Additionally, the introduction of human stem cells into the brains of living great apes, whether during prenatal or postnatal stages, is prohibited. Breeding animals that have received human pluripotent stem cells is also expressly forbidden. The Fourth Schedule delineates restricted practices, allowing limited research on human eggs and embryos, certain types of human-animal combination embryos, and the introduction of human stem cells into prenatal or postnatal animal subjects, with specific exceptions for certain studies involving immunodeficient mice solely for analysing teratoma induction. These provisions aim to uphold ethical standards in biomedical research while still permitting some avenues for scientific exploration.

3.4.4 Guidelines

In 2015, the BAC consolidated all of its past recommendations on the regulations of human biomedical research into a single document, *Ethics Guidelines for Human Biomedical Research* (hereinafter, Guidelines 2015) (Bioethics Advisory Committee, 2015). The main purpose of these guidelines is to provide guidance and facilitate researchers and ethics committees in carrying out best practices to ensure ethical conduct in human biomedical research in Singapore. There were three biomedical research areas specifically addressed in the Guidelines 2015, namely biobanking and research involving human biological materials, human genetic research, and human stem cell research. In light of the advancements in biomedical sciences and major developments in the regulatory system in Singapore, especially with the establishment of the Human Biomedical Research Act 2015, the BAC undertook a review of its guidelines in 2021 to ensure that it remains an up-to-date guiding rule in the country, resulting in the Ethics Guidelines for Human Biomedical Research (2021 Revised Edition).

The 2021 revised edition includes the issues involving cerebral organoids that can be used in disease modelling, drug testing for precision medicine, or regenerative medicine. The BAC is of the opinion that *in vitro* research using human cerebral organoids should be permitted as it does not pose additional ethical, legal, or social issues and therefore does not require any additional safeguards. However, *in vivo* use of such organoids falls within the restricted research regulations. The relevant provisions on human stem cell research as provided by the 2021 Revised Edition are highlighted as follows:

Exemption from review for non-contentious research

In Singapore, human stem cell research that is deemed non-contentious, specifically research utilising established pluripotent stem cell lines confined to cell cultures or standard laboratory practices involving animals, is exempted from extensive review processes. This pragmatic approach allows researchers to engage in foundational studies that are low risk while ensuring that more ethically sensitive research receives the scrutiny it warrants. For all other human stem cell research, full or expedited reviews by Institutional Review Boards (IRBs) are mandatory. This protocol allows for a meticulous evaluation of potential ethical concerns, particularly in studies involving human eggs, embryos, or combinations of human and animal materials, which require additional oversight from the Ministry of Health (MOH).

Procurement of biological materials

The procurement of biological materials—including gametes, embryos, foetal tissue, and somatic cells—must adhere to strict guidelines established in Part V of the revised guidelines. This ensures that all materials, whether sourced domestically or imported, are obtained ethically and responsibly. Establishing clear protocols helps to mitigate risks of exploitation and supports societal confidence in stem cell research practices.

Ethical considerations in animal research

Research that incorporates human embryonic stem cells (hESCs), induced pluripotent stem cells (iPSCs), or any form of pluripotent stem cells into animals is subject to heightened ethical scrutiny. Researchers must focus on preventing the creation of entities in which human sentience or consciousness could conceivably arise. This precaution underscores a commitment to ethical considerations that respect both human dignity and animal welfare. Additionally, animals into which hESCs or iPSCs are introduced must not be permitted to breed, thereby containing the influence of human cells within a controlled environment and further minimising ethical concerns associated with such interventions.

Limitations on human cytoplasmic hybrid embryos

Singapore's guidelines strictly prohibit the development of human cytoplasmic hybrid embryos beyond 14 days in vitro, as well as their implantation into humans or animals. This regulation reflects a cautious approach to potentially contentious ethical issues surrounding hybridisation and the implications of such entities in scientific research and medicine.

Requirements for clinical trials involving pluripotent stem cells

When research involves introducing human embryonic stem cells, pluripotent cells, or derived products into humans, it is mandated to align with the rigorous standards set for clinical trials for cell-based products as outlined by the Health Sciences Authority (HSA). Approval from the HSA is required prior to the initiation of such studies. Furthermore, IRBs are tasked with ensuring several stringent criteria are met proposals must undergo scientific review by qualified committees, there must be substantial evidence of safety and efficacy from pre-clinical trials, participants must receive comprehensive information regarding risks and the source of cells, and informed consent should be collected unobtrusively, free from coercion or undue pressures.

Exclusions for innovative or experimental uses

It is important to note that these guiding rules do not encompass innovative or experimental applications of stem cells within clinical practice, which fall outside the purview of the Bioethics Advisory Committee (BAC). This delineation acknowledges the need for flexibility in clinical settings to adapt to novel therapeutic approaches while maintaining ethical standards.

Respecting conscientious objections

The guidelines also affirm the right of clinical and research personnel to abstain from participating in stem cell research to which they have a conscientious objection, particularly regarding human embryonic stem cells or human-animal combination studies. This provision protects the moral integrity of researchers and clinicians, ensuring that they are not compelled to compromise their personal beliefs while participating in scientific advancements.

3.5 Overview of Malaysia's governance framework

3.5.1 The landscape of stem cell industry

Academic and research institutions

As with many other countries, Malaysia also recognised the importance of human stem cell research in developing stem cell-based therapy for many degenerative diseases. Moreover, stem cell technology is also viewed as a significant driver of Malaysia's economic growth, especially given Malaysia's aspiration to be the hub of medical tourism in the region (Bt Hj Idrus et al., 2015). It was reported by the Academy of Sciences Malaysia that there were approximately 110 stem cell researchers in the country when its advisory report was published in 2013 (*Advisory Report on Stem Cells: Ageing and Regenerative Medicine*). It is expected that the number may have changed over the past decade.

These researchers are affiliated with public research universities such as Universiti Malaya, Universiti Kebangsaan Malaysia, Universiti Putra Malaysia, and Universiti Sains Malaysia as well as private universities including the International Medical University, Universiti Tunku Abdul Rahman, International Islamic University, Nottingham University, and Monash University. Some of them are affiliated with the Institute of Medical Research, a public research entity under the purview of the federal government, and international entities based in Malaysia, such as Stempeutics.

Clinical applications and trials

While there are significant developments in clinical trials and applications in other countries including the United Kingdom and Singapore, it can be said that Malaysia is still lagging behind (Imran et al., 2022). However, there are a number of clinical applications reported in Malaysia. One of the established stem cell therapies in Malaysia is hematopoietic stem cell transplantation (HSCT). The Malaysian Stem Cell Registry was established in 2000 with the specific aim to promote and recruit bone marrow and peripheral stem cell donors. The first paediatric HSCT was performed by the University of Malaya Medical Centre in 1987 followed by adult HSCT in 1993. As of 2020, it was reported that there are a total of 13 hospitals including private, government, and teaching hospitals throughout the country offering HSCT. In addition, the Cord Blood Bank Unit was established in 2003 given the fact that scientists can also harvest hematopoietic stem cells from umbilical cord blood as an alternative to bone marrow and to help address the shortages for patients who require HSCT but do not have suitable family donors. Later in 2014, the National Stem Cell Coordinating Center was established as a one-stop centre to coordinate and facilitate HSCT involving recipients and unrelated donors (Saidon et al., 2020). Other hospitals that are well known for offering stem cell-based therapy are Hospital Ampang Clinical Stem Cell Services, which focuses more on blood cancer treatment, and the UKM Medical Centre's Cell Therapy Centre, which was founded in 2005 that provides cell-based therapy for blood disorders, cancers, bone marrow diseases, and degenerative diseases.

Other types of stem cell therapies are being investigated in clinical trials for conditions such as diabetes, autism, osteoarthritis, and heart disease. There are also ongoing clinical trials that use unmatched donor umbilical cord-derived mesenchymal stem cells to treat knee articular cartilage defects and the use of MSC for anti-ageing (Wu et al., 2019). Nonetheless, the applications of stem cell treatment are still uncommon in the country due to the lack of evidence-based clinical trials.

Collaboration and international engagement

The Malaysian stem cell industry has witnessed increasing interest from both local and international investors. Several startups specialising in stem cell technology and regenerative medicine have emerged. Companies like Stem-Life Berhad have established themselves in the market, offering umbilical cord blood banking and stem cell-derived therapies. In addition, the Malaysian Stem Cell Therapy Working Group was also established as a network involving different stem cell providers in Klang Valley that bring together multi-disciplined specialists who provide research-driven regenerative medicine (Malaysia, 2012).

3.5.2 Advisory body

The proposal from the Ministry of Science, Technology and Innovation (MOSTI) to establish a National Bioethics Council aimed at fostering ethical standards in science and technology in Malaysia was approved by the Cabinet on 9 July 2010. This Council serves as an advisory body to address bioethical challenges across various domains, including environmental, social, health, cultural, legislative, and religious issues arising from advancements in science and technology.

Upon its formation, the National Bioethics Council was composed of members appointed by the MOSTI Minister. It included ten experts with backgrounds in bioethics, genetics, medical pharmaceuticals, and related fields, along with fourteen representatives from government ministries, agencies, and non-governmental organisations (NGOs). To facilitate its core functions, three working committees were established under the Council, tasked with reporting and making recommendations on relevant activities.

The primary focuses of the National Bioethics Council include:

a. Disseminating information on bioethical issues to the public to foster greater awareness.
b. Promoting bioethical principles in science and technology through research and development and assessing their societal impacts.
c. Examining the legal, ethical, and social implications related to research involving human biology.

The terms of reference for the Council are as follows:

a. To advise and mainstream bioethics among policymakers, researchers, industry stakeholders, educators, students, practitioners, and the public.
b. To recommend strategies for enhancing awareness of ethical issues among researchers, educators, policymakers, and industry representatives, particularly concerning the latest developments and best practices in the life sciences, including medicine, biotechnology, genetics, and biology.
c. To disseminate information and promote awareness of bioethics across all facets of life through dialogue and collaboration among stakeholders involved in bioethical issues.
d. To establish subcommittees as needed to advance the Council's activities.
e. To prepare and publish reports and recommendations.

Since its inception, there is no available documentation indicating whether the Council has specifically addressed the ethical challenges associated with human stem cell research, particularly the use of human embryos and derived stem cells and cell lines for research purposes within the local context. Some of the Council's activities have primarily focused on the ethical considerations surrounding the use of animals in laboratory experiments. In 2012, the Council organised its inaugural bioethics seminar in collaboration with Universiti Malaya. This event aimed to provide a foundational introduction to bioethics, explore the relationship between bioethics and society, share information across various fields, and discuss pertinent bioethical issues both nationally and internationally. The seminar covered three main bioethical areas: ethical concerns related to modern biotechnology in agriculture, animal experimentation, and human research in general. Since then, there has been no report on other activities carried out by the Council.

3.5.3 Laws

In contrast to several countries that have established comprehensive legal frameworks specifically addressing human embryo research, Malaysia currently lacks dedicated legislation that comprehensively governs all aspects related to the utilisation of human embryos in research. This legislative gap necessitates that researchers navigate existing laws that are not exclusively focused on this domain; rather these laws encompass various ethical guidelines and the involvement of ethics committees, which may result in notable gaps and ambiguities in oversight.

Some existing laws, such as the Human Tissue Act 1974 and the Medical Act 1971, pertain to ethical practices regarding human tissue. However, these laws do not provide exhaustive regulations specific to human embryo research and primarily address broader issues related to medical research and tissue handling. For instance, the Human Tissue Act 1974 delineates a legal framework for the removal, use, and storage of human tissue intended for transplantation and medical research (Human Tissue Act, 1974). While it underscores the necessity of obtaining informed consent for the use of human tissues, it conspicuously lacks explicit reference to human embryos.

Review bodies, such as the Medical Research and Ethics Committee (MREC), are tasked with evaluating research proposals involving human subjects, including studies related to embryos. Although these committees provide critical oversight, they function within the constraints of existing laws rather than under specific legislation dedicated to embryo research. Given that Malaysia currently lacks specific legislation directly regulating human embryo research, there is an increasing recognition of the necessity for a comprehensive legal framework to adequately address the unique ethical and scientific considerations inherent in this field (Bin Abdul Aziz et al., 2022). This urgent need for regulatory reform will be explored in greater detail in the subsequent chapter.

3.5.4 Guidelines

Guidelines for Stem Cell Research and Therapy 2006

The 2006 Guidelines stipulate the utilisation of adult stem cells, fetal tissue obtained from legally performed terminations of pregnancy, non-human stem cell lines, and embryonic stem cell lines, all of which are permitted (Ministry of Health, 2006). However, these guidelines prohibit the creation of embryos through *in vitro* fertilisation (IVF) or somatic cell nuclear transfer (SCNT), also known as cell nuclear replacement (CNR) in the United Kingdom, for research purposes. The only embryos authorised for research are "sample or excess embryos" resulting from IVF treatments. In this context, it can be argued that Malaysia's approach is comparatively more restrictive than that of the United Kingdom and Singapore.

Additionally, even though the usage of excess embryos is permissible, researchers are still required to seek guidance from religious authorities, highlighting their significant role in shaping Malaysia's policies in this domain. This is particularly pertinent given that Islam is the official religion of the country, and fatwas are explicitly integrated into the Guidelines. For instance, the fatwa issued by the Malaysian National Fatwa Council stipulates that therapeutic human cloning is permitted if it serves medical purposes, specifically for the regeneration of cells or the replacement of damaged organs, and if it adheres to the stipulations of Syari'ah. However, it also categorically states that stem cells derived from SCNT-created embryos are not permitted based on the principle of sadd al-zarai (blocking the means of evil), which aims to block potential avenues for ethical misconduct.

Given these ethical concerns, the Guidelines mandate that stem cell research be conducted with the highest medical and ethical standards. However, the 2006 Guidelines fall short of providing clear definitions of these standards, rendering them somewhat incomplete. The Institutional Review Board (IRB) and Institutional Ethics Committee (IEC) are tasked with overseeing stem cell research, requiring review and approval prior to the initiation of any research. Nonetheless, the absence of clearly articulated medical and ethical standards could lead to variability in the assessment measures employed by these review bodies, introducing further complications. Fortunately, this issue has been addressed with the advent of a new set of guidelines.

In August 2009, the Medical Development Division of the Ministry of Health, in collaboration with several universities, organised a Stem Cell Research and Therapy Seminar. The Honourable Liow Tiong Lai, the Former Minister of Health of Malaysia, underscored the necessity for the nation to recognise stem cell research and therapy as a rapidly evolving global enterprise fraught with controversial issues that must be comprehensively understood and not underestimated. The Minister further emphasised the government's commitment to encouraging and supporting the involvement of local scientists and clinicians in stem cell research, notwithstanding the surrounding controversies. At this seminar, the National Guidelines for Stem Cell Research and Therapy 2009 (hereinafter referred to as the 2009 Guidelines) were introduced as a framework for conducting both stem cell research and therapy in Malaysia.

The National Guidelines for Stem Cell Research and Therapy 2009

Similar to the earlier guidelines, the 2009 Guidelines also permit human embryonic research (embryonic stem cell research) on the condition that the 14-day rule is adhered to and explicitly prohibits the creation of human embryos (Ministry of Health, 2009). Additionally, these guidelines expand the scope of permitted research by allowing the formation of human admixed embryos provided that such embryos are not maintained or developed beyond 14 days or until the primitive streak appears, whichever occurs first. Compared to the 2006 Guidelines, the 2009 Guidelines offer more comprehensive and detailed guidance regarding stem cell research.

The 2006 Guidelines only mandate that the Institutional Review Board (IRB) and Institutional Ethics Committee (IEC) approve stem cell research, granting these bodies the authority to evaluate potential research proposals without providing any specific points of reference. As previously discussed, this lack of standardisation may lead to varying assessment approaches among different IRBs and IECs, potentially creating an inequitable situation that fails to satisfy the research community at large. In contrast, the 2009 Guidelines establish appropriate medical and ethical standards, explicitly stating that the "Guidelines are to be used as a point of reference" for the IRB and IEC.

The 2009 Guidelines require that: (i) the use of human embryos for deriving stem cells to be a voluntary decision free from any influence by investigators; (ii) the attending physician responsible for infertility treatment not to be the same individual proposing to use human embryonic stem cells (hESCs); (iii) the prohibition of any financial compensation for the donation of blastocysts; (iv) informed consent to be obtained from donors at the time of donation, as well as at the initiation of any specific research, with donors retaining the right to withdraw consent until the blastocysts are used in cell line derivation. Furthermore, the 2009 Guidelines underscore the importance of individual autonomy by specifying the information required during the informed consent process.

However, the Guidelines do not confer full authority upon the IRB and IEC to make final determinations regarding the eligibility of research proposals. According to Paragraph 3 of the 2009 Guidelines, "the National Stem Cell Research and Ethics Sub-Committee . . . retains the right to review any research proposal as necessary". This provision indicates that the National

Stem Cell Research and Ethics Sub-Committee possesses the authority to review research approved by the IRB and IEC at any time.

Regarding medical standards, the 2009 Guidelines stipulate that laboratories conducting stem cell research must: (i) adhere to good laboratory practices and comply with General Medical Practice (GMP) as mandated by the National Pharmaceutical Control Bureau (NPCB); (ii) ensure that any products intended for commercialisation are certified as GMP compliant; and (iii) verify that imported stem cells are GMP certified and registered with the NPCB.

Similar to the 2006 Guidelines, the 2009 Guidelines maintain the same list of permitted and prohibited sources of stem cells. It is noteworthy that both sets of guidelines permit the use of embryonic stem cells derived exclusively from surplus embryos. With respect to the creation of embryos, the 2006 Guidelines specifically prohibit their generation through assisted reproductive technology (ART), or SCNT, a stance that may be overly restrictive given the rapid advances in technology and the potential development of new methods for embryo creation. This raises a critical question: should novel methods, not explicitly mentioned in the Guidelines, also be prohibited? Recognising the swift evolution of this technological landscape, the 2009 Guidelines are drafted in a more comprehensive and dynamic manner. They explicitly state in Paragraph 10 that the creation of an embryo "by any means", and "not limited to" ART and SCNT, is prohibited. The phrases "by any means" and "not limited to" strengthen the prohibition against any methods for creating human embryos, thereby reflecting the Guidelines' responsiveness to ongoing advancements in reproductive technology and ethical considerations.

National Assisted Reproductive Technology Policy 2021

In addition to the guidelines governing stem cell research, the Ministry of Health has established a National Assisted Reproductive Technology Policy (Ministry of Health, 2021). Paragraph 6 of the Policy is particularly relevant to this discussion, as it uses gametes and embryos, for research, placing significant emphasis on the necessity of obtaining consent from couples undergoing ART treatment regarding the use of embryos for research purposes, and approval from Medical Review and Ethics Committee (MREC) and National Medical Research Register (NMRR). Couples are required to specify a maximum storage duration (up to five years) and must outline the procedures for disposing of their gametes or embryos in the event of their demise or incapacity to alter or revoke their joint consent. Additionally, according to Paragraph 11 of the national guidelines on assisted reproduction established by the Malaysian Medical Council (2006), they must provide explicit instructions concerning the storage and disposal of embryos, including their use in research. This underscores that obtaining consent is a critical requirement before gametes or embryos can be stored or utilised for research.

With regard to research, the national guidelines permit the use of surplus embryos, provided that approval has been obtained from the Ministry of Health and that the research adheres to the 14-day limit stipulated in the existing guidelines. This provision aligns with both the 2006 and 2009 Guidelines.

3.5.5 Other relevant guidelines

National Standards for Stem Cell Transplantation 2018

The Ministry of Health published the second edition of the NSSCT in 2018. This document sets forth essential standards for stem cell transplantation, addressing the collection, processing, storage, release, transportation, infusion, and disposal of hematopoietic stem cells and therapeutic cells. It also outlines the quality management measures for these cells as well as specific protocols for returning stem cells and therapeutic products in cases where transplantation does not occur or when there are surplus products after the procedure. The guidelines require proper documentation to be maintained for returned products and this includes tracking information as well as storage condition details (Ministry of Health, 2018).

National Guidelines for Hematopoietic Stem Cell Therapy 2009

Considering the critical importance of hematopoietic stem cell therapy, which is actively practised in Malaysia, the Ministry of Health has issued guidelines to delineate the essential standards for clinical facilities performing this procedure. The guidelines emphasise several key aspects of this emerging intervention, including the competency of personnel, accepted indications for transplantation, assessment protocols for donors and recipients, and the requisite quality management policies to ensure the safety of both patients and donors (Ministry of Health, 2009).

National Standards for Cord Blood Banking and Transplantation 2019

This guideline was developed by the Ministry of Health in collaboration with field experts. The 2019 edition of this guideline establishes the minimum standards for cord blood banks in Malaysia and emphasises the importance of standardised laboratory practices across all phases of cord blood management. It also advocates for a comprehensive quality management approach to produce cells that are of high quality and viable to ensure a successful cord blood-derived stem cell transplantation (Ministry of Health, 2019).

Guidance Document and Guidelines for Registration of Cell and Gene Therapy Products (CGTPs) in Malaysia 2022

These guidelines were published by the National Pharmaceutical Regulatory Agency (NPRA) and should be considered in conjunction with the second edition of the Good Tissue Practice Guideline issued by the National Pharmaceutical Control Bureau. The primary objective of these guidelines is to establish the standards and requirements necessary for the registration of cell and gene therapy products (CGTPs). Currently, CGTPs in Malaysia are classified into two categories: low-risk and high-risk, each with specific regulatory criteria. With the implementation of these guidelines, the registration and enforcement of high-risk CGTPs have become mandatory as of 1 January 2021 (National Pharmaceutical Regulatory Agency, 2022).

3.6 Conclusion

In conclusion, the landscape of international regulations governing stem cell research reflects a complex interplay of principles designed to protect human rights and dignity while fostering scientific advancement. The Convention on Human Rights and Biomedicine emphasises the significance of human dignity and informed consent, yet it leaves substantial ambiguities regarding the moral and legal status of human embryos. This lack of clarity has resulted in varied interpretations among its signatories. Similarly, the Universal Declaration on Bioethics and Human Rights reiterates the importance of human dignity without explicitly defining how these principles should apply to human embryos.

In the United Kingdom, the governance framework, anchored by the Human Fertilisation and Embryology Act, facilitates a comprehensive and progressive approach to stem cell research, particularly concerning the use of human embryos. This framework consistently balances ethical considerations with the need for scientific exploration. It is further supported by policy guidance from prominent advisory bodies, including the Warnock Committee and the Nuffield Council on Bioethics. Moreover, the evolving regulatory landscape, as evidenced by the Human Fertilisation and Embryology Act 2008 and the establishment of the UK Stem Cell Bank, underscores a commitment to ethical oversight while promoting innovation and collaboration across various sectors. This legal development illustrates the United Kingdom's dedication to protecting human embryos through stringent regulatory measures, such as a licencing system and ongoing monitoring.

Turning to Singapore, their governance framework for stem cell research embodies a strong commitment to advancing this promising field while upholding ethical standards and societal responsibilities. The pioneering work of scientists like Ariff Bongso has positioned Singapore among the leading nations in stem cell research, catalysing significant government support, investment, and infrastructure development. To facilitate research advancement, Singapore has also established a proactive and integrated governance framework that balances the potential benefits of stem cell therapies with the essential need to protect human rights and dignity. The legislation governing all forms of human biomedical research places specific emphasis on the use of human embryos and gametes. Notably, this important statutory framework is complemented by guidelines and advisory bodies that ensure ethical considerations remain central to scientific exploration.

In contrast, Malaysia's governance framework faces unique challenges, particularly the absence of a comprehensive legal framework for embryo research. Despite ongoing efforts in stem cell applications and a burgeoning research community, Malaysia's restrictive guidelines, shaped by ethical and religious considerations, underscore the complexities of advancing stem cell research within a diverse societal context. The establishment of bodies like the National Bioethics Council signifies an acknowledgement of the need for ethical oversight; however, considerable gaps remain in the regulatory framework. As Malaysia navigates the challenges and opportunities in this field, collaboration, innovation, and a steadfast commitment to ethical integrity will be vital in shaping the future of regenerative medicine in the country. Malaysia stands to benefit from the experiences of the United Kingdom and Singapore, which will be explored in the subsequent chapter.

References

Academy of Science Malaysia & U. P. M. Institute of Gerontology. (2013). *Advisory report on stem cells: Ageing and regenerative medicine*. https://www.akademisains.gov.my/asm-publication/stem-cells-medicine/

Belew, K. L. (2003). Stem cell division: Abortion law and its influence on the adoption of radically different embryonic stem cell legislation in the United States, the United Kingdom, and Germany. *The Texas International Law Journal*, *39*, 479.

Beyleveld, D. (2001). *Human dignity in bioethics and biolaw*. Oxford University Press.

Beyleveld, D., & Brownsword, R. (2001). *Human dignity in bioethics and biolaw*. Oxford University Press.

Bin Abdul Aziz, M. F., Morrison, M., & Kaye, J. (2022). Creative regulatory practices to develop stem-cell technology: The way forward for Malaysia. *Regenerative Medicine*, *17*(2), 91–105.

Bioethics Advisory Committee. (2002). *Ethical, legal and social issues in human stem cell research, reproductive and therapeutic cloning: A report from the Bioethics Advisory Committee, Singapore*. Author.

Bongso, A., Fong, C.-Y., Ng, S.-C., & Ratnam, S. (1994). Fertilization and early embryology: Isolation and culture of inner cell mass cells from human blastocysts. *Human Reproduction*, *9*(11), 2110–2117.

Bt Hj Idrus, R., Abas, A., Ab Rahim, F., & Saim, A. B. (2015). Clinical translation of cell therapy, tissue engineering, and regenerative medicine product in Malaysia and its regulatory policy. *Tissue Engineering Part A, 21*(23–24), 2812–2816.

Chief Medical Officer's Expert Group Reviewing the Potential of Developments on Stem Cell Research and Cell Nuclear Replacement to Benefit Human Health, Office of the CMO, UK. (2000). *Stem Cell Research: Stem Cell Research: Medical Progress with Responsibility: Executive Summary*. Cloning, *2*(2), 91–96.

Colman, A. (2008). Stem cell research in Singapore. *Cell, 132*(4), 519–521.

Council of Europe. (1997). Convention for the Protection of Human Rights and Dignity of the Human Being with regard to the Application of Biology and Medicine: Convention of Human Rights and Biomedicine 1997. https://rm.coe.int/168007cf98

Curle, A. J., Barnes, J. L., Owen, R., Barker, R. A., El Haj, A., Forbes, S. J., Ghevaert, C., Oreffo, R. O., Rose, F. R., & Stevens, M. M. (2024). A decade of progress: Achievements and future challenges for regenerative medicine research in the United Kingdom. *Journal of Immunology and Regenerative Medicine*, 100078, 24–25. https://www.sciencedirect.com/science/article/pii/S2468498824000027.

Health Products Act 2007 (Singapore).

Health Products (Clinical Trials) Regulations 2016 (Singapore).

Hottois, G. (2000). A philosophical and critical analysis of the European Convention of Bioethics. *The Journal of Medicine and Philosophy: A Forum for Bioethics and Philosophy of Medicine, 25.*

Human Biomedical Research Act 2015 (Singapore).

Human Biomedical Research (Restricted Research) Regulations 2017 (Singapore).

Human Cloning and Other Prohibited Practices Act 2004 (Singapore).

Human Fertilisation and Embryology Act 1990 (United Kingdom).

Human Fertilisation and Embryology Act 2008 (United Kingdom).

Human Tissue Act 1974 (Malaysia).

Imran, S. A., Hamizul, M. H. A., Khairul Bariah, A. A. N., Wan Kamarul Zaman, W. S., & Nordin, F. (2022). Regenerative medicine therapy in Malaysia: An update. *Frontiers in Bioengineering and Biotechnology, 10*, 789644.

International Society for Stem Cell Research. (2021). Guidelines for Stem Cell Research and Clinical Translation 2021. https://www.isscr.org/guidelines

Jackson, E. (2006). *Medical Law: Text, Cases and Materials*. Oxford University Press.

Kuo, L. (1996). Lessons learned from Great Britain's human fertilization and embryology act: Should the United States regulate the fate of unused frozen embryos. *The Loyola of Los Angeles International and Comparative Law Journal, 19*, 1027.

Malaysia Ministry of Health. (2012). *Press statement Minister of Health, Malaysia, 1st National Stem Cell Congress*. Author.

Malaysia Ministry of Health. (2023). *National guidelines for haemopoietic stem cell therapy*. Author.

Ministry of Health, Malaysia. (2006). Guidelines for Stem Cell Research and Therapy 2006. https://www.moh.gov.my/index.php/database_stores/store_view/70?mid=1321

Ministry of Health, Malaysia. (2009). Guidelines for Stem Cell Research and Therapy 2009. https://www.moh.gov.my/index.php/database_stores/store_view/70?mid=1321

Ministry of Health, Malaysia. (2018). National Standards for Stem Cell Transplantation 2018. https://www.moh.gov.my/index.php/database_stores/store_view/70?mid=1321

Ministry of Health, Malaysia. (2019). National Standards for Cord Blood Banking and Transplantation 2019. https://www.moh.gov.my/index.php/database_stores/store_view/70?mid=1321

Ministry of Health, Malaysia. (2021). National Assisted Reproductive Technology Policy 2021. https://www.moh.gov.my/index.php/database_stores/store_view/70?mid=1321

Morgan, R. (2007). A tight fit? Deficiencies in the human fertilisation and embryology (research purposes) regulations 2001. *Statute Law Review, 28*(3), 199–217.

National Pharmaceutical Regulatory Agency, Malaysia. (2022). Guidance Document and Guidelines for Registration of Cell and Gene Therapy Products (CGTPs) in Malaysia 2022. https://npra.gov.my/index.php/en/guideline-bio/1527314-guidance-document-and-guidelines-for-registration-of-cell-and-gene-therapy-products-cgtps-in-malaysia-2.html

National Standards for Stem Cell Transplantation. (2018).

Nuffield Council on Bioethics. (2000). *Stem cell therapy: The ethical issues*. Author. https://www.nuffieldbioethics.org/publications/stem-cells

Nuffield Council on Bioethics. (2017). *Human embryo culture: Discussions concerning the statutory time limit for maintaining human embryos in culture in the light of some recent scientific developments*. Author. https://www.nuffieldbioethics.org/publications/time-limits-on-maintaining-human-embryos-in-research

Pattison, S. (2009). *Medical law and ethics* (2nd ed.). Sweet and Maxwell.

R (on the application of Quintavalle) v Secretary of State for Health, [2003] 2 AII E.R. 113.

Regina v. Secretary of State for Health (Respondent) ex parte Quintavalle (on behalf of Pro-Life Alliance) (Appellant), [2003] UKHL 13.

Rossi, E. (2009). The exemption that confirms the rule: Reflections on proceduralism and the UK hybrid embryos controversy. *Res Publica, 15*, 237–250.

Saidon, N., Anuar, N. A., Meng, C. K., Chuan, O. T., Mui, T. S., Gin, G. G., Fadilah, S., Ariffin, H., Peng, L. H., & Lee, C. L. (2020). Evolution of hematopoietic stem cell transplant programs in Malaysia. *Blood Cell Therapy, 3*(3), 44.

Singapore Bioethics Advisory Committee. (2015). Ethics Guidelines for Human Biomedical Research 2015. https://www.bioethics-singapore.gov.sg/files/publications/reports/ethics-guidelines-for-human-biomedical-research-full-report.pdf

Singapore Bioethics Advisory Committee. (2021). Ethics Guidelines for Human Biomedical Research (2021 Revised Edition). https://file.go.gov.sg/bacethicsguidelines2021-a5.pdf

Sivarajah, S., Raj, G. S., Mathews, A. J. V., Sahib, N. B. E., Hwang, W. S., & Crook, J. M. (2010). The generation of GLP-grade human embryonic stem cell banks from four clinical-grade cell lines for preclinical research. *In Vitro Cellular & Developmental Biology-Animal*, *46*, 210–216.

Tay, H. G., Andre, H., Chrysostomou, V., Adusumalli, S., Guo, J., Ren, X., Tan, W. S., Tor, J. E., Moreno-Moral, A., & Plastino, F. (2023). Photoreceptor laminin drives differentiation of human pluripotent stem cells to photoreceptor progenitors that partially restore retina function. *Molecular Therapy*, *31*(3), 825–846.

The Human Fertilisation and Embryology (Research Purposes) Regulations 2001 (United Kingdom).

Thomson, J. A., Itskovitz-Eldor, J., Shapiro, S. S., Waknitz, M. A., Swiergiel, J. J., Marshall, V. S., & Jones, J. M. (1998). Embryonic stem cell lines derived from human blastocysts. *Science*, *282*(5391), 1145–1147.

UK Stem Cell Bank Steering Committee. (2010). Code of Practice for the Use of Human Stem Cell Lines. https://assets.publishing.service.gov.uk/government/uploads/system/uploads/attachment_data/file/1182116/Code_of_Practice_for_the_Use_of_Human_Stem_Cell_Lines__2010__-_amended_August_2023.pdf

UNESCO. (2005). Universal Declaration on Bioethics and Human Rights 2005. https://www.unesco.org/en/ethics-science-technology/bioethics-and-human-rights?hub=387

Universal Declaration on Bioethics and Human Rights. (2005).

Warnock, M. (1985). *A question of life: The Warnock report on human fertilisation and embryology*. London: Basil Blackwell.

Wilmut, I., Schnieke, A. E., McWhir, J., Kind, A. J., & Campbell, K. H. (1997). Viable offspring derived from fetal and adult mammalian cells. *Nature*, *385*(6619), 810–813.

Wu, K.-C., Chang, Y.-H., Liu, H.-W., & Ding, D.-C. (2019). Transplanting human umbilical cord mesenchymal stem cells and hyaluronate hydrogel repairs cartilage of osteoarthritis in the Minipig model. *Tzu Chi Medical Journal*, *31*(1), 11–19.

Yap, L., Chong, L. Y., Tan, C., Adusumalli, S., Seow, M., Guo, J., Cai, Z., Loo, S. J., Lim, E., & Tan, R. S. (2023). Pluripotent stem cell-derived committed cardiac progenitors remuscularize damaged ischemic hearts and improve their function in pigs. *NPJ Regenerative Medicine*, *8*(1), 26.

4 Regulatory response to ethical issues

4.1 Introduction

In the evolving landscape of biomedical ethics, the moral status of human embryos remains a contentious and multifaceted issue. With implications that resonate throughout legal, religious, and cultural frameworks, differing regulatory perspectives play a crucial role in shaping research practices across nations. This chapter aims to investigate the regulatory views regarding the moral status of human embryos in three distinct jurisdictions: the United Kingdom, Singapore, and Malaysia and how these jurisdictions respond to the ethical issues surrounding this sensitive research field.

As discussed in Chapter 2, varying interpretations concerning when human embryos should be granted moral status underscore the complexity of this debate. While international regulations provide limited clarity, the diverse approaches adopted by the United Kingdom, Singapore, and Malaysia reveal significant ideological divides. This section builds on the analysis presented in Chapter 3, which outlined under-studied jurisdictions in the context of human stem cell research, specifically focusing on the use of human embryos for research purposes.

The policies enacted within these jurisdictions illustrate a shared belief that early-stage human embryos do not possess the same moral status as fully developed human beings. However, this perspective also considers the strong religious sentiments, especially in Malaysia, towards the need to protect the sanctity of life. Consequently, the moral status of embryos is not merely a scientific or philosophical inquiry, but a matter deeply intertwined with local ethical values and religious beliefs.

Furthermore, the chapter will explore how regulatory frameworks, such as the 14-day rule, serve as temporal limits and moral compromises that reflect a gradual ascension in moral status as human embryos develop. While the United Kingdom and Singapore adopt a more permissive stance allowing both the creation and use of human embryos in research, Malaysia's approach is comparatively conservative, permitting research solely on surplus embryos. This divergence invites critical examination of the underlying ideological

DOI: 10.4324/9781003583479-4

values, expert influences, and governmental structures that shape these regulatory frameworks.

As we navigate through the differing approaches to the moral status of human embryos adopted by these jurisdictions, this chapter ultimately seeks to provide insight into whether Malaysia should reconsider its cautious regulatory stance in light of the advancements and moral imperatives surrounding human embryonic research. Through a comprehensive analysis, we can better understand the complexities of ethical governance in this rapidly evolving field and propose strategic considerations for future legislative development in Malaysia.

4.2 Regulatory views on the moral status of human embryos: United Kingdom, Singapore, and Malaysia

As discussed in Chapter 2, there are diverse perspectives on the moral status of human embryos, particularly concerning when they should be granted full moral status. This complex issue is not clearly addressed by international regulations, as highlighted at the beginning of Chapter 3. The latter part of Chapter 3 analyses the regulatory approaches adopted by under-studied jurisdictions regarding human stem cell research, particularly the use of human embryos for research purposes.

It can be argued that the policies implemented in the United Kingdom, Singapore, and Malaysia suggest that human embryos in these jurisdictions do not hold the same moral status as fully developed human beings, especially in the early stages of development. This is noteworthy given the demography of the local societies, particularly in Malaysia, that still maintain strong religious beliefs, whereby some groups assert that life begins at conception.

Furthermore, the positions taken by these jurisdictions tend to align with the moral view that there is no definitive moment when a human embryo becomes a person, implying that its moral status increases gradually as development advances (Ehrich et al., 2007). This perspective is evident in the regulatory approaches of the United Kingdom, Singapore, and Malaysia, which emphasise the emergence of a primitive streak and the incorporation of the 14-day rule. These serve as temporal limits and moral compromises that recognise the potential for human embryos to achieve a form of personhood.

However, it is important to note that Malaysia's stance is somewhat more cautious compared to those of the United Kingdom and Singapore regarding the moral status of human embryos. While the United Kingdom and Singapore apply the same moral compromise for both the use of surplus embryos and the creation of human embryos for research, Malaysia restricts its regulations to only the use of surplus human embryos. Whether Malaysia's approach differs significantly in moral terms requires further discussion among relevant experts. Nonetheless, the following section attempts to briefly address this question.

4.3 The differing ideological values

4.3.1 The use of human embryos for research

As previously noted, the application of the 14-day rule in regulating the use and creation of human embryos for research purposes in Malaysia differs from that in the United Kingdom and Singapore. While both the United Kingdom and Singapore have adopted a pragmatic approach by instituting the 14-day rule to allow both the use of surplus embryos and the creation of new embryos specifically for research, Malaysia has taken a more cautious regulatory stance, whereby only surplus embryos can be used for research. This divergence can be attributed to the differing backgrounds of the advisory bodies that have influenced policy recommendations in these jurisdictions.

Historically, as discussed in Chapter 2, the Human Fertilisation and Embryology (HFE) Act of 1990 in the United Kingdom was significantly shaped by the report of the Warnock Committee. In Singapore, the Cabinet accepted all recommendations made by the Singapore Bioethics Advisory Committee, which were subsequently incorporated into existing laws, including the proposition to adopt the United Kingdom's approach as a foundational model, which explains the shared regulatory approach between these jurisdictions. In contrast, Malaysia's national guidelines for regulating stem cell research and therapy integrate the entirety of the fatwa produced by the National Fatwa Committee. It is important to note that while the Warnock Committee and the Singapore Bioethics Advisory Committee comprised prominent experts from a range of fields, the Malaysian National Fatwa Council is composed primarily of religious leaders and Islamic scholars.

Consequently, one could argue that there exists a substantial divergence in the ideological principles that underpin the perspectives of these entities, particularly concerning the creation of embryos for research. The 2009 Malaysian Guidelines reflect the position articulated by the Fatwa Council, which maintains a conservative stance on therapeutic cloning, particularly regarding the creation of embryos through somatic cell nuclear transfer (SCNT), in order to mitigate potential ethical transgressions. In Malaysia, the creation of embryos has never been sanctioned; only surplus embryos generated through *in vitro* fertilisation (IVF) are permitted for embryonic research, with the creation of human embryos categorically prohibited based on the Fatwa Council's religious doctrines. This regulatory framework is heavily influenced by conservative religious perspectives. In contrast, the United Kingdom and Singapore have opted for a more permissive regulatory environment that prioritises medical benefits in their decision-making processes.

Importantly, Malaysia also has a National Bioethics Council, which consists of relevant experts from diverse backgrounds rather than being predominantly religious in orientation. However, it is noteworthy that the Council was not involved in the development of the national guidelines, as it was established in 2010 after the guidelines were first introduced in 2006 and revised in 2009. This raises the question of whether Malaysia's regulatory stance would differ if the National Bioethics Council had been given the mandate to make policy recommendations for this ethically complex issue.

4.3.2 Would Malaysia in the future allow the creation of human embryos for research?

Therapeutic cloning through somatic cell nuclear transfer (SCNT), also referred to as cell nuclear replacement (CNR) in the United Kingdom, is deemed by scientists and researchers as a pivotal approach for advancing stem cell research (UK Parliamentary Office of Science and Technology, 2002). This method offers a preferable alternative to utilising surplus embryos as sources of pluripotent stem cells. In Malaysia, the prohibition against the creation of human embryos raises concerns that research involving human embryonic stem cells (HESCs) may be considerably more restricted than in other countries that permit the generation of embryos for research purposes. Such prohibitions may be perceived as contradictory to the commitments articulated in the 2006 and 2009 Guidelines, which reflect the Malaysian government's aspiration to promote human stem cell research.

The restrictive framework governing human embryonic research in Malaysia could hinder progress, particularly if the availability of surplus human embryos is limited and alternative sources of HESCs remain inaccessible due to the existing ban on embryo creation. Rather than imposing stringent regulations that could obstruct research advancement, Malaysian authorities might consider implementing substantive regulatory measures, including licencing requirements and enhanced oversight for embryonic research, akin to those in the United Kingdom (Bin Abdul Aziz et al., 2022). These measures would serve as a framework to effectively regulate both the utilisation of surplus human embryos and the generation of new embryos for research. Presently, such regulatory measures are absent in Malaysia, and the ramifications of this lack are explored in another section of this chapter.

Moreover, the ethical justification underpinning the 14-day rule, endorsed by the Fatwa Council concerning the use of surplus human embryos, merits re-evaluation to potentially facilitate the creation of embryos. This modification could mitigate concerns regarding a slippery slope leading to reproductive cloning. However, the rationale for not expanding the time limit to encompass the creation of human embryos has not been adequately articulated in the fatwa. Engaging in academic discourse would be beneficial to gain a more nuanced understanding of the Fatwa Council's position.

Recent advances by UK scientists have demonstrated the profound benefits of human embryonic research, exemplified by the successful generation of red blood cells, which has the potential to alleviate global blood shortages and provide critical assistance to millions of patients in need. Nonetheless, should the supply of surplus human embryos become insufficient in Malaysia in the future, a crucial question arises: will Malaysian authorities, including the Ministry of Health (MOH) and the Fatwa Council, maintain or reconsider their prohibition? This ethical dilemma is particularly salient in light of observations made in Chapter 3, where certain Muslim scholars advocate for human embryo research on the grounds of its moral imperative to save lives, a principle sanctioned by Islamic teachings and, according to some interpretations, regarded as a communal obligation or known as *fard kifayah*.

It can be posited that the prohibition on the creation of human embryos in Malaysia is primarily a consequence of the current availability of surplus human embryos for research purposes, thus negating the immediate need for new embryo creation. However, should circumstances shift, such that no viable alternatives exist, the Malaysian regulatory bodies, in conjunction with the Fatwa Council, may need to reevaluate their stance on human embryo creation to fulfil the objectives of stem cell research. Such a reconsideration may become increasingly necessary given advancements in *in vitro* fertilisation (IVF) techniques, which could lead to a decreased need for a significant number of surplus embryos. In such a scenario, ethical frameworks, such as the 14-day rule and other stringent regulatory parameters, would likely be upheld to avert unethical practices.

Additionally, the limitations may also stem from the nature of the current stem cell research activities in Malaysia. At present, there is no official registry providing insights into the state of embryonic research in the country. A report from 2013 indicated that only a limited number of embryonic stem cell studies were undertaken, with the majority of research focused on adult stem cells, including mesenchymal stem cells, dental pulp stem cells, cancer stem cells, and hematopoietic stem cells (Academy of Sciences Malaysia, 2013). This context may lead to the conclusion that there is no urgent necessity to revise Malaysia's regulatory approach. This perspective is further bolstered by empirical studies involving key stakeholders, wherein a local scientist and a member of the advisory council suggested that it would be more advantageous for Malaysia to prioritise more mature and feasible stem cell technologies, such as induced pluripotent stem cells, over embryonic stem cells (Bin Abdul Aziz et al., 2018). Also, limited funding in this domain, along with the complexities associated with embryonic research, may contribute to the overall lack of interest among stem cell scientists in the country to pursue embryonic research or the use of embryonic stem cells.

However, given that more than a decade has elapsed since the 2013 report, there is an imperative need to assess the current developments in stem cell research in Malaysia. It is essential to ascertain whether there has been an increase in embryonic stem cell research and, if not, to identify the contributing factors. If there is indeed interest among local scientists to pursue embryonic research and utilise human embryonic stem cells, the current policy prohibiting the creation of human embryos may hinder research endeavours and jeopardise Malaysia's position relative to leading nations in human stem cell research, such as the United Kingdom and Singapore. Consequently, Malaysia risks falling behind in keeping pace with ongoing advancements in this critical field of research (Bin Abdul Aziz et al., 2022).

4.4 Regulatory infrastructures: comparison between the United Kingdom, Singapore, and Malaysia

4.4.1 Statutory body

It has been observed that the UK government relies on the Human Fertilisation and Embryology Authority (HFEA) as the statutory body responsible for functions such as licencing research and overseeing activities related to gametes and embryos. It can be argued that the HFEA is a good model for a statutory body. It comprises experts with diverse backgrounds in medical, scientific, social, legal, and religious disciplines, as stipulated by Schedule 1, Paragraph 4 of the "Human Fertilisation and Embryology Act" (1990). According to Lee and Morgan, the inclusion of such varied expertise within an authorized body responsible for the review of research is intended to ensure that the consensus reached is independent of any singular medical-scientific perspective, which is essential in ensuring public interest is protected (Morgan, 2007).

Nonetheless, critics contend that the existing regulatory framework is fragmented and overly complex, potentially jeopardising the United Kingdom's position as a global leader in this domain (Bell & Devaney, 2007). An examination of the United Kingdom's regulatory landscape in the preceding chapter demonstrates that different authorities govern distinct stages of human embryonic stem cell (hESC) research, highlighting a fragmented regulatory environment. This section outlines the various stages of hESC research, along with the relevant authoritative bodies and legislation involved, to illustrate this fragmentation.

The initial stage of human embryonic research involves the utilisation of live human embryos, from which hESCs are derived. This process is governed by the Human Fertilisation and Embryology Act 1990 (as amended by the Human Fertilisation and Embryology Act 2008) and falls under the jurisdiction of the HFEA, encompassing the period from the use of human embryos to the derivation of hESCs. However, the subsequent stage, which focuses on the utilisation of established stem cell lines for further research, is not regulated by the HFE Act or the HFEA. Instead, this phase is overseen by the UK Stem Cell Bank Steering Committee, which provides non-binding guidance on the storage and use of these cell lines. It is important to note that research involving hESCs conducted solely for basic laboratory purposes does not attract the same level of regulatory scrutiny. Conversely, when stem cells are used for research intended for human application, this falls under a different legal framework, specifically the Human Tissue (Quality and Safety) Regulations

2007, and is regulated by the Human Tissue Authority (HTA). Critics argue that the United Kingdom's regulatory framework is not only fragmented and complex but also exhibits overlapping jurisdictions (Lee & Morgan, 2001).

In contrast to the United Kingdom, Singapore has implemented a more straightforward regulatory framework governing this area of research. Although Singapore's Bioethics Advisory Committee (BAC) recommended establishing a statutory body similar to the United Kingdom's model, the government opted not to enact specific legislation governing the use of human embryos and eggs. Instead, it introduced legislation that governs all forms of biomedical research, incorporating specific provisions for sensitive research involving human eggs, human embryos, and human-animal combination embryos, as detailed in the "Human Biomedical Research (Restricted Research) Regulations" (2017). These regulations confer the authority to review and approve such research to institutional review boards and the Director of Health, illustrating that Singapore lacks a statutory body with specific functions equivalent to the HFEA; instead, the IRBs and the Ministry of Health play active roles in overseeing sensitive research.

Similarly, Malaysia lacks a designated statutorily established body specifically tasked with overseeing sensitive research involving human embryos. Current national guidelines necessitate approval from an institutional review board and the National Stem Cell Research and Ethics Sub-Committee. However, it is noteworthy that this sub-committee does not regulate basic research, and only governs research projects affiliated with the Ministry of Health. This suggests a potential regulatory gap between basic and clinical research as well as between public and private sector oversight.

Establishing an independent body with statutory authority and a broader mandate to comprehensively oversee all research involving human embryos, human eggs, and admixed embryos would be advantageous. However, given Malaysia's status as a developing nation, funding poses a significant concern when considering the creation of such a body (Bin Abdul Aziz et al., 2022). Furthermore, in light of pressing issues, such as the inadequate infrastructure necessary to meet the increasing demands for public healthcare, prioritisation of public health concerns may overshadow the governance of this ethically sensitive research. Consequently, it is unlikely that Malaysia would allocate funding specifically to regulate this area in the same manner as that adopted by the United Kingdom.

Nonetheless, it remains crucial for Malaysia to reevaluate its current regulatory framework to address the identified gaps. Rather than simply emulating the United Kingdom's model, Malaysia could adopt the approach taken by Singapore, whereby the Ministry of Health, through its director, possesses the regulatory authority to oversee all research involving human embryos, eggs, and admixed embryos across both public and private sectors. This is facilitated by legislation governing all forms of biomedical research, a legal framework currently absent in Malaysia. Therefore, it is imperative for Malaysia to consider enacting similar legislation, an issue further elaborated in the subsequent section.

4.4.2 Substantive requirement: licencing and monitoring

As previously noted, the Human Fertilisation and Embryology Authority (HFEA) in the United Kingdom is the body responsible for determining whether research should be granted a licence, as mandated by the Human Fertilisation and Embryology Act 1990 (as amended). The HFEA is also empowered to establish sub-committees, one of which is the HFEA licencing committee. This committee has adopted a stringent licencing procedure that encompasses five substantive steps:

- The applicant must first contact the HFEA to determine whether they need to apply for a new licence or to renew an existing one. For a new licence, approval from the Local Research Ethics Committee is required; for renewals, the applicant may contact the HFEA Regulation Department directly.
- A completed application must then be submitted to the HFEA Compliance Department, accompanied by an administrative fee.
- The HFEA Compliance Department will conduct peer reviews of the submitted application.
- If the peer reviews are deemed satisfactory, the HFEA will conduct an inspection of the proposed research premises.
- Finally, the application, peer reviews, and the inspectors' report will be presented to the HFEA Research Licencing Committee for consideration.

Furthermore, the HFEA's licencing requirements mandate that scientists in the United Kingdom comply with the specific criteria when deriving human embryonic stem cell lines including the deposition of each derived stem cell line in the UK Stem Cell Bank. This ensures that all cell lines available for research purposes from the UK Stem Cell Bank are ethically sourced.

In contrast, Singapore's regulatory framework does not explicitly impose a licencing requirement; instead, it relies on approvals granted by Institutional Review Boards (IRBs) and the Director General, as mandated by its law. The provisions outlined in Part 4 of the Human Biomedical Research Act 2015 articulate the duties of IRBs and the Director. This Act empowers IRBs to review any proposed biomedical research, allowing them the discretion to approve, require modifications for approval, or disallow the research altogether. Additionally, IRBs possess the authority to exempt certain biomedical research from the review process or to expedite its review. However, research involving human embryos, ova, and human-animal chimeras—categorised as restricted research—cannot be exempted from review or subjected to expedited processes.

The 2017 Regulations stipulate that, for restricted research, in addition to IRB approval, endorsements from an Institutional Animal Care and Use Committee (if it involves animals) and the Director's approval are also legally required, particularly for studies initiated after 1 November 2017. For research commenced before this date but not completed by it, the relevant research institution must inform and obtain satisfaction from the Director regarding the proper conduct and IRB approval of the study. If expected completion occurs after 1 November 2018, the research must receive approval from the IRB, the Institutional Animal Care Committee (where applicable), and the Director.

In Malaysia, there is no designated regulatory body akin to the HFEA that specifically oversees and licences human embryonic research. According to the 2009 Guidelines, all stem cell research applications must be ethically and scientifically approved by the respective Institutional Review Board and/or Institutional Ethics Committee, mirroring the approach taken in Singapore. However, Malaysia's national guidelines do not explicitly include the role of the Director General of Health in the approval process. Instead, the ethics sub-committee is authorised to review any research at any time, without the requirement for mandatory committee approval. Notably, there is limited information regarding how these bodies fulfil their responsibilities in regulating the use of human embryos for research purposes in Malaysia.

In comparison to the United Kingdom, Malaysia's regulatory framework appears relatively lenient, as there are no enforceable regulations ensuring that all forms of research involving human embryos are held to high standards. The absence of licencing requirements and the lack of mandatory approval from the Ministry of Health (MOH) as a regulatory body further underscore this disparity. Conversely, while Singapore also lacks a formal licencing requirement, it imposes stringent oversight based on the types of human materials used in research. While the use of pluripotent stem cells is exempt from extensive review processes, all other types of stem cell research must undergo a full or expedited review by an IRB. Any research involving human eggs, embryos, or combinations of animal-human materials necessitates additional oversight from the MOH—a measure that is currently lacking in Malaysia.

Since ethical approval in Malaysia is practised only at the institutional level, questions arise regarding the standardisation of regulatory practices across the country and the rigour of the review processes. One might also wonder about oversight: do ethics committees track research activities that have been approved? How is the use of human embryos monitored to prevent unnecessary utilisation and redundancy in research projects nationwide? Given that the guidelines apply only to research conducted by public institutions or those affiliated with public bodies, who oversee the use of human embryos in the private sector to ensure compliance with the 14-day rule? Moreover, how can it be ensured that the embryos used for research are ethically sourced?

It could be argued that Malaysia would benefit from implementing a more comprehensive oversight system, such as licencing provisions similar to those in the United Kingdom, to regulate both public and private sectors and address the regulatory gaps identified earlier (Bin Abdul Aziz et al., 2022). Such measures would enhance the reputation of research activities in Malaysia, facilitating collaborative work for researchers. Unlike ethical approvals from IRBs or IECs, which may involve questions about standardisation and rigour, a statutory licencing system would require all research to undergo a strict licencing process before approval. Furthermore, this approach could increase awareness among researchers regarding existing regulations; it has been reported that some researchers are unaware of the national guidelines. Additionally, a licencing system could serve as a compliance strategy, helping researchers adhere to regulations by ensuring they engage with regulators before commencing their research.

If Malaysia is unable to introduce a licencing system due to resource and capacity limitations, an alternative would be to emulate Singapore's approach by imposing legal obligations on the MOH and its relevant offices to assume a more proactive regulatory role. This recommendation is particularly pertinent given concerns raised by key stakeholders in Malaysia, who have indicated that there is insufficient practical oversight of activities in the stem cell research sector. They have noted a perceived inadequacy of enforcement in non-clinical research, particularly regarding informed consent and whether consent was obtained for stem cells used in subsequent research beyond the scope of original consent—a concern exacerbated by the lack of monitoring (Bin Abdul Aziz et al., 2018).

Consequently, the current system in Malaysia raises significant concerns regarding proper oversight, potentially allowing for unethical conduct that could tarnish the reputation of stem cell technology, and the researchers committed to advancing this field ethically. Reference can be made to the findings of Zhang (2014), which identify concerns regarding the ethical integrity of research governance in China. It was reported that "ethical oversight was loosely undertaken through local institutions. In the absence of a nationally recognized directive, skepticism arose internationally about the quality of Chinese laboratories' working standards and regulatory supervision" (2011, p. 201). This scenario underscores the critical role that jurisdictional regulation plays in fostering confidence among reputable institutions at the global level. Concerns shared by a key stakeholder in Malaysia emphasised personal challenges in procuring research samples from other institutions due to uncertainties surrounding Malaysia's current policy on the protection of embryonic stem cells.

In light of these observations, it is essential to consider the Chinese experience and the personal accounts shared by stakeholders when seeking to enhance the current regulatory system in Malaysia. Establishing a designated regulatory body would facilitate stringent rule enforcement and monitoring. As argued by Kian and Leng (2005, p. 297), "for an effective legal framework, human stem cell research should be regulated and monitored in accordance with relevant ethical considerations". This enhancement would align the regulatory framework with global best practices, thereby enabling local researchers to engage in collaborative efforts with their international counterparts.

Moreover, should Malaysia decide to implement a licencing system or a properly regulated approval process involving the MOH, such measures could govern the creation of human embryos for research purposes, should Malaysia consider this possibility in the future. Malaysia could learn from the United Kingdom's model, which permits the creation of human embryos for research on a case-by-case basis, conditional on licencing requirements and rigorous monitoring. Such an approach serves dual purposes: facilitating advancements in embryonic research when necessary and safeguarding the special status of human embryos by providing them with appropriate legal protections. Currently, one could argue that Malaysia's regulatory approach does not effectively serve either of these objectives.

4.4.3 Substantive requirement: the 14-day rule

As shown previously, the United Kingdom adopts a liberal approach through a consistently controlled permissive stance regarding the approval of all forms of human embryonic research, underpinned by the ethical framework provided by the 14-day rule. This rule has been rigorously applied as a fundamental prerequisite for any proposed research involving human embryos. As previously discussed, the 14-day rule serves not only as an ethical justification for utilising human embryos in research but also for their creation as well as for the generation of human-admixed embryos. Initially recommended by the Warnock Committee, the 14-day time limit has since received legislative recognition and has been a substantive requirement enshrined in the Human Fertilisation and Embryology Act 1990 (as amended).

Numerous countries globally, including Singapore and Malaysia, have adopted this 14-day rule. Similar to the United Kingdom, Singapore does not limit the application of this time frame solely to the use of surplus embryos for research purposes. Singapore does not explicitly prohibit the creation of human embryos for research, provided that research institutions do not conduct restricted studies on human embryos that are more than 14 days old from the moment of their creation, excluding any period during which embryonic growth is suspended. This limitation has been given legal effect in Singapore through its incorporation into the Regulations 2017.

In contrast, the application of the 14-day rule in Malaysia is significantly more restrictive, as it is confined to the use of surplus embryos only. This limitation stems from the prevailing perspective of the national fatwa, which seeks to mitigate potential unethical practices that might arise if the creation of embryos for research were permitted. Given that Malaysia is predominantly a Muslim country, with Islam as the official religion, the national fatwa reflects this religious context and warrants a reconsideration of the Islamic perspective on the moral status of human embryos.

As noted in Chapter 2, moderate Islamic scholars generally assert that ensoulment occurs either 40 or 120 days post-fertilisation. Consequently, the pragmatic 14-day rule established by the UK Warnock Committee appears more cautious when juxtaposed with these moderate Islamic views. This discrepancy raises pertinent questions regarding the decisions made by the National Fatwa Committee:

First, one might question why the Fatwa Committee did not opt to implement a 40-day or 120-day rule in regulating the use of human embryos in Malaysia. Adopting such a framework would position Malaysia in a markedly different category on the international regulatory landscape, which may not be well-received by countries adhering to the 14-day standard. Given that 14 days is currently recognised as the international benchmark, it is imperative for Malaysia to align with this standard; failing to do so may diminish Malaysia's reputation and hinder its researchers' opportunities for collaboration with international peers.

Second, it could be argued that if Malaysia is to adhere to international standards, it should also consider adopting the approaches taken by the United Kingdom and Singapore, which permit both the use of surplus embryos and the creation of new embryos. However, it is crucial to recognise that the fatwa not only reflects Islamic perspectives but also incorporates viewpoints from other religious groups in the country with more restrictive stances. Thus, the decision to apply the 14-day rule solely to surplus *in vitro* fertilisation (IVF)-created human embryos was ultimately a pragmatic response to the sensitive nature of this issue and the diverse opinions among religious factions. While it remains essential to adhere to the internationally accepted standard of 14 days, ongoing debates, as discussed in Chapter 3, persist regarding the potential extension of this time limit to 28 days. This matter should be addressed by Malaysia's National Bioethics Council. Currently, it is not known whether the Council has engaged in deliberations on these ethical issues within the local context.

Nevertheless, it is vital for Malaysia to consider the advancement of research in this field, as well as the future necessity of creating human embryos for research purposes. The rationale behind the current prohibition, grounded in the avoidance of unethical practices as outlined by the Fatwa Council, could support the adoption of a legislative framework similar to that of the United Kingdom and Singapore. Presently, the application of the 14-day rule in Malaysia lacks binding legal authority, as it has not been codified within the country's legislation. Consequently, it can be posited that the absence of legally enforced regulations, coupled with insufficient monitoring mechanisms, undermines this rationale; within the existing regulatory environment, even the use of surplus embryos may lead to unethical conduct without proper oversight, unlike the rigorous enforcement observed in the United Kingdom and Singapore.

4.4.4 Substantive requirement: consent

In both the United Kingdom and Singapore, obtaining consent is a critical requirement for any research seeking licencing from the Human Fertilisation and Embryology Authority (HFEA) in the United Kingdom and approval from the Director of Health in Singapore. The Human Fertilisation and Embryology (HFE) Act 1990 (as amended) emphasises the necessity of obtaining written consent for the use or storage of human embryos and human admixed embryos. This consent may be retracted, provided that the embryos have not yet been utilised for the approved research purposes.

Similarly, the importance of consent is highlighted in the governance of biomedical research in Singapore. Sections 6 to 14 of the Human Biomedical Research (HBR) Act 2015 (as revised) specifically address consent and include the following key elements: (i) the legal responsibility of researchers to execute an appropriate informed consent process in writing; (ii) the requirement to obtain consent from various parties, including adults, minors, individuals lacking capacity, and for the removal of tissue from deceased individuals; (iii) a detailed outline of the information that must be communicated to individuals prior to obtaining their consent; (iv) stipulations under which an Institutional Review Board (IRB) may waive the consent requirement; and (v) guidelines regarding the withdrawal of consent.

In Malaysia, the principle of informed consent is also being enforced, as articulated in the 2009 Guidelines and the Code of Practice. Paragraph 10 of the 2009 Guidelines offers guidance on how consent should be managed for the donation of gametes or blastocysts for research. This indicates that all the jurisdictions discussed recognise the critical importance of consent as a substantive requirement that must be strictly adhered to. However, the rigour of consent requirements presents a disparity: the standards in the United Kingdom and Singapore are more stringent compared to those in Malaysia. In the United Kingdom, for instance, consent must be documented in writing and signed by the consenting individual, a requirement mirrored in Singapore. Contrastingly, the 2009 Guidelines and the Assisted Reproduction Guidelines in Malaysia do not specify such formal requirements. This raises the possibility that Malaysia should reconsider its current regulations and potentially adopt approaches similar to those of the United Kingdom and Singapore to enhance its regulatory framework.

Furthermore, the lack of a national licencing system and review or approval processes at the national level in Malaysia raises questions about the consistency of informed consent practices among various Institutional Review Boards (IRBs) and ethical review committees (IECs) at the institutional level. Informed consent is a fundamental principle that ensures respect for the autonomy of research participants or donors. Given that sensitive research in Malaysia is currently governed solely by non-binding national guidelines, which may not extend to the private sector, the promotion of autonomy in this area is indeed questionable. The existing system relies on individual researchers, particularly in the private sector, to navigate their own moral and ethical considerations which may not be a reliable approach in practice.

To enhance the enforcement and legality of consent requirements, Malaysia might consider establishing more robust legal frameworks similar to those in the United Kingdom and Singapore. This would ensure that the principles governing informed consent are not only upheld but are also legally binding, further protecting the rights of research participants and donors.

4.4.5 Sanction

Both the United Kingdom and Singapore have established stringent requirements, as highlighted in the preceding sections, which must be met by research communities to ensure that human embryonic research is conducted within an ethical framework in these jurisdictions. The United Kingdom's permissive stance on the use of human embryos and oocytes for research purposes is characterised as a consistent approach throughout its scientific advancements, a viewpoint supported by the legal developments discussed in Chapter 3. Despite the reviews and amendments to the law, it retains this permissive stance, allowing all forms of human embryonic research while concurrently upholding restrictive substantive regulatory requirements. To enforce compliance, any research project that disregards these substantive requirements is considered an offence under Section 41 of the HFE Act 1990 (as amended), with convicted individuals subject to legal penalties, including imprisonment, fines, or both.

Legal prosecution through a sanctioning strategy is not exclusive to the United Kingdom; it is also a common approach adopted by other nations, including Singapore, which legislates in this area. Section 31(4) of its BHR Act 2015 (as revised) stipulates that any person who contravenes Subsections (1) or (3) shall be guilty of an offence and, upon conviction, liable to a fine, imprisonment, or both. This sanctioning strategy arguably enhances the significance of the substantive requirements, particularly the 14-day rule.

As previously noted, Malaysia has also adopted the same 14-day rule, which researchers must adhere to before commencing proposed research. However, the enforcement of this rule in Malaysia is notably lax and lacks legal robustness, as there are no statutory penalties imposed for violations. In contrast, violations of this rule in the United Kingdom and Singapore result in criminal liability, as outlined in their respective legislation. In Malaysia, since the 14-day rule is merely a guideline issued by the MOH and not a legally binding statute, there is no legal recourse to convict individuals who conduct embryonic research without a licence or ethical approval or fail to comply with substantive requirements.

This disparity illustrates that while researchers in the United Kingdom and Singapore face possible imprisonment for conducting research without the necessary licences or for ignoring regulatory requirements, researchers in Malaysia may only have their work halted, with no legal penalties imposed. Thus, although Malaysia adopts a more restrictive approach concerning the use of human embryos for research, this is not reflected in its regulatory measures. In contrast, the regulatory frameworks in the United Kingdom and Singapore incorporate licencing and approval systems at the national level as compliance strategies, alongside sanctioning measures as a final recourse for non-compliance.

Given the controversial and ethically challenging nature of human embryonic research, it would be ethically prudent for Malaysian regulators to adopt both compliance and sanctioning strategies. Such measures would not only prevent unethical conduct but also provide the necessary legal authority to enforce sanctions when required.

4.4.6 Advisory body and public debate

The rapid advancement of new and emerging technologies—such as biotechnology, nanotechnology, genomics, and stem cell research—brings with it an array of complex ethical dilemmas. If these technologies develop without proper oversight, they can potentially lead to significant risks and profound social ramifications. To effectively navigate these intricate challenges authorities and policymakers often lack the requisite expertise and, therefore, depend on guidance from expert panels. Thus, the role of advisory bodies becomes essential in facilitating informed political decision-making related to ethically contentious technologies and helping policymakers establish appropriate regulatory frameworks. These entities are regarded as fundamental components of "good governance" in the regulation of emerging technologies and represent a progressive strategy for ensuring that research and innovation proceed responsibly.

For instance, Europe has seen the emergence of a network of ethics advisory bodies over recent decades, including the German Ethics Council, the Italian National Bioethics Committee, the Danish Council of Ethics, the Belgian Advisory Committee on Bioethics, and the Finnish National Advisory Board, among others. These bodies provide institutionalised policy advice on ethically sensitive issues. As highlighted in Chapter 3, similar organisations such as the Warnock Committee in the United Kingdom, the UK Nuffield Bioethics Council, and the Singapore Bioethics Committee fulfil this role by addressing complex ethical dilemmas and advising the government. Their contributions have significantly influenced regulatory practices and helped establish formal guidelines within their respective jurisdictions. Notably, some European ethics advisory bodies have observed that their findings have been explicitly referenced in legislation or court rulings, albeit often without direct acknowledgement of their contributions.

Moreover, these advisory bodies play a vital role in fostering governance that is both transparent and responsive to the imperatives of responsible research and innovation. They employ various mechanisms for public engagement, involving a diverse range of stakeholders to address the controversies surrounding the ethical dimensions of new scientific fields. This approach utilises public communication, consultation, and participatory strategies. The UK Nuffield Bioethics Council, for example, exemplifies an inclusive method of public engagement by regularly publishing the outcomes of its deliberations, conducting public discussions, facilitating deliberative workshops, and organising educational seminars. In addressing the moral and ethical implications of hybrid embryo research, the United Kingdom has adopted a practical approach that reflects the sentiments of key stakeholders, including the public, by providing forums for discussion and platforms for expressing concerns—whether in support of or against hybrid embryo research.

Despite their importance, these advisory bodies face criticism regarding the sufficiency of expertise among their members to tackle complex ethical issues effectively. As a result, some bodies may only provide knowledge that informs action without making explicit recommendations to policymakers. However, this discussion does not delve into the operational challenges faced by these ethics bodies, focusing instead on their critical role in an increasingly ethically complex research environment.

In contrast to the approaches taken by the United Kingdom and Singapore, Malaysia's regulatory framework concerning the use of human embryos is significantly influenced by a fatwa committee, which aligns more closely with religious sentiments than with expert bodies like the Nuffield Council and Singapore's Bioethics Advisory Committee, which integrate diverse expertise and perspectives. This lack of inclusivity may arise from the fact that Malaysia's National Bioethics Council was established after the introduction of national guidelines, raising questions about how the nation's stance might differ if the National Bioethics Council had participated in formulating these guidelines. Notably, little information is publicly available regarding the policy advice produced by the Council in this sensitive area. Moving forward, it is essential for the Council to actively provide ethical guidance on critical issues, such as whether Malaysia should allow the creation of human embryos for research purposes.

To enhance its effectiveness, the Malaysian Council should adopt the model established by the Nuffield Council and the Singapore Bioethics Advisory Committee, which engages not only with experts but also with the public through various channels and activities. Given Malaysia's multiracial and multireligious composition, fostering informed and open public discourse is crucial. Encouraging interfaith and intercultural dialogue among individuals from diverse cultural and religious backgrounds is vital for allowing communities to engage with pertinent issues and collaboratively seek guidelines that reflect the majority perspective.

Malaysia must acknowledge that traditional decision-making practices, where policymakers enact regulations without active involvement from experts and the public, are no longer adequate in contemporary society—especially regarding the societal implications and acceptable impacts of emerging sciences and technologies.

4.5 Strategic considerations for legislation on human embryonic research in Malaysia

The examinations of the substantive requirements outlined in the preceding sections have consistently highlighted the necessity for Malaysia to consider endowing the measures currently outlined in existing guidelines with legal effect akin to that observed in the United Kingdom and Singapore. However, it is imperative for Malaysian policymakers to weigh the advantages and disadvantages of such an initiative.

Given the reported lack of awareness among researchers and insufficient enforcement, one could argue that establishing a governance framework underpinned by legislative systems—alongside mandated bodies or entities dedicated to rigorous enforcement—would constitute an appropriate strategy. Jurisdictions with well-defined legislative frameworks, such as the United Kingdom and Singapore, benefit from more comprehensive mechanisms for enforcing regulations, contrasting sharply with Malaysia's current lack of formal legislation. For example, the statutory and appointed authorities in the United Kingdom and Singapore are empowered to oversee regulated activities and possess the legal authority to act against non-compliance. In this regard, while Malaysia relies on non-binding rules, jurisdictions with legislative frameworks enforce regulations on all entities operating within this regulated domain, regardless of whether they belong to the public or private sector.

Nevertheless, it is crucial to acknowledge the potential concerns associated with prevailing attitudes toward legislation, which might lead to excessively prescriptive or over-inclusive rules, thereby resulting in over-regulation. Kian and Leng assert that "any proposed laws and regulations must be sufficiently flexible to permit an adequate response to the rapid advancements in science and biotechnology" (Kian & Leng, 2005). It is of paramount importance to facilitate, rather than obstruct, significant and deserving research in human stem cell technology and therapeutic cloning, which holds tremendous promise for curative cell therapy treatments.

While recognising the essential role of legislation, it is equally important to appreciate the significance of guidelines. Given that rules enshrined in law are not self-explanatory, clear interpretations are often necessary, which can be provided through guiding documents. As discussed in Chapter 3, both the United Kingdom and Singapore govern this research through legal frameworks while simultaneously employing guidelines. It is essential for Malaysia to regard its national guidelines as dynamic documents that should be updated in accordance with scientific advancements and the emerging issues therein. The last revision of the national guidelines occurred in 2009, indicating that a thorough reassessment is overdue.

Regarding whether Malaysia should emulate the United Kingdom's approach, which primarily governs the use of human embryos and gametes, or follow Singapore's model, which regulates all forms of human biomedical research while specifying regulations for embryos and oocytes, this matter requires further deliberation among the various key stakeholders within the country. Given that Malaysia is a small, low- to middle-income country with relatively limited capacity to invest in regulatory infrastructure, this reality is reflected in the current regulatory system, which is characterised by minimal guidance from regulators and inadequate monitoring and enforcement mechanisms. As argued by Bin Abdul Aziz, it is important for Malaysia to consider the "national homekeeping" approach (Sleeboom-Faulkner et al., 2016) that strives to reconcile the expectations for appropriate conduct established by scientific authorities in developed nations with the need for policies tailored to Malaysia's unique economic, health, and scientific contexts—factors significantly influenced by local resources and demands (Bin Abdul Aziz et al., 2018). Thus, it is imperative for Malaysia to ascertain the most effective strategy for balancing the prevention of moral harm arising from research involving human embryos and oocytes, the protection of public safety, and the flexibility necessary to foster scientific advancement.

4.6 Conclusion

The exploration of the regulatory views on the moral status of human embryos in the United Kingdom, Singapore, and Malaysia reveals a complex landscape shaped by diverse ethical, cultural, and religious contexts. As highlighted in the preceding sections, these jurisdictions exhibit differing approaches to human embryonic research, driven by varying interpretations of when moral status is conferred to embryos and the regulations governing their use.

The policies in place reflect a consensus that human embryos, particularly in early stages, do not possess the same moral status as fully developed human beings. The application of the 14-day rule serves as a significant marker of this understanding, allowing for regulated research within a framework that acknowledges the potential for personhood development over time. Yet, Malaysia's regulatory stance appears more cautious, confining its provisions to surplus embryos and reflecting the influence of religious doctrines on its ethical and moral landscape.

In comparing the regulatory frameworks of the United Kingdom and Singapore, which embrace a more permissive model allowing for the creation and use of embryos, Malaysia's restrictions underscore a deeper cultural conservatism stemming from its unique religious and ethical milieu. This divergence illustrates the necessity for Malaysia to engage in critical discussions about its regulatory future, particularly in terms of adapting its guidelines to reflect advances in science and to remain competitive in the realm of biomedical research.

Moving forward, it is crucial for Malaysian policymakers to consider the establishment of a more robust legal framework akin to those in the United Kingdom and Singapore. Such a framework would not only enforce compliance and provide clarity but also facilitate ethical research practices that respect both scientific advancement and moral considerations. The integration of expert opinions from diverse fields of study as well as public debate is essential in fostering a regulatory environment that is both ethically sound and conducive to innovation.

Furthermore, there is an imperative need for the Malaysian National Bioethics Council to play an active role in reassessing existing guidelines, ensuring they evolve in alignment with scientific progress and societal values. Open dialogues and collaborative efforts among stakeholders will be pivotal in shaping a balanced approach that harmonises ethical, cultural, and scientific imperatives in human embryonic research.

Ultimately, as Malaysia navigates the intricacies of regulating human embryonic research, it must remain vigilant in safeguarding public interest while nurturing its scientific ambitions. The journey toward developing a scientifically progressive and ethically responsible framework is not only a national necessity but also a moral imperative that supports the advancement of medicine and the health of communities both locally and globally.

References

Academy of Sciences Malaysia. (2013). *Advisory report on stem cells: Ageing and regenerative medicine*. Author.

Bell, L., & Devaney, S. (2007). Gaps and overlaps: Improving the current regulation of stem cells in the UK. *Journal of Medical Ethics*, *33*(11), 621–622. https://pmc.ncbi.nlm.nih.gov/articles/PMC2598104/pdf/621.pdf

Bin Abdul Aziz, M. F., Morrison, M., & Kaye, J. (2018). Regulating human stem cell research and therapy in low-and middle-income countries: Malaysian perspectives. *New Genetics and Society*, *37*(1), 2–20.

Bin Abdul Aziz, M. F., Morrison, M., & Kaye, J. (2022). Creative regulatory practices to develop stem-cell technology: The way forward for Malaysia. *Regenerative Medicine*, *17*(2), 91–105.

Ehrich, K., Farsides, B., Williams, C., & Scott, R. (2007). Testing the embryo, testing the fetus. *Clinical Ethics*, *2*(4), 181–186. https://pmc.ncbi.nlm.nih.gov/articles/PMC2312333/pdf/ukmss-1532w.pdf

Human Biomedical Research (Restricted Research) Regulations 2017 (Singapore).

Human Fertilisation and Embryology Act 1990 (United Kingdom).

Human Fertilisation and Embryology Act 2008 (United Kingdom).

Kian, C. T. S., & Leng, T. S. (2005). The Singapore approach to human stem cell research, therapeutic and reproductive cloning. *Bioethics*, *19*(3), 290–303.

https://onlinelibrary.wiley.com/doi/abs/10.1111/j.1467-8519.2005.00442.x?sid=nlm%3Apubmed

Lee, R. G., & Morgan, D. (2001). *Human fertilisation and embryology: Regulating the reproductive revolution*. Blackstone Press.

Morgan, R. (2007). A lack of foresight? Jurisdictional uncertainties in the regulatory interface between the HFEA, the UK Stem Cell Bank and beyond. *Legal Studies*, *27*(3), 511–535.

Sleeboom-Faulkner, M., Chekar, C. K., Faulkner, A., Heitmeyer, C., Marouda, M., Rosemann, A., Chaisinthop, N., Chang, H.-C. J., Ely, A., & Kato, M. (2016). Comparing national home-keeping and the regulation of translational stem cell applications: An international perspective. *Social Science & Medicine*, *153*, 240–249.

UK Parliamentary Office of Science and Technology. (2002). *Stem cell research*. Author.

Zhang, J. Y. (2011). Scientific institutions and effective governance: a case study of Chinese stem cell research. *New Genetics and Society*, *30*(2), 193–207.

5 The way forward for Malaysia

5.1 Overall conclusions

This book aims to offer a comprehensive overview of the multifaceted field of human stem cell research (hSCR), with a particular emphasis on the promising potential of human embryonic stem cells (hESCs) as precursors for tissue regeneration and therapeutic advancements. It begins by elucidating the unique properties of stem cells, particularly the pluripotency exhibited by hESCs, which enables these cells to differentiate into a wide array of cell types. These cells are regarded as the "gold standard" in the scientific community, proving invaluable in addressing significant medical challenges, including degenerative diseases and organ repair.

As countries like the United Kingdom, Singapore, and Malaysia advance their research in hSCR, ethical controversies surrounding the use of human embryos complicate public acceptance and policy formation. This book analyses the ethical dilemmas, focusing specifically on the moral status of embryos and how this complex ethical question is addressed at both the international level and within the under-studied jurisdictions. It primarily investigates how Malaysia approaches the contentious issue of human embryo usage in stem cell research compared to more experienced countries like the United Kingdom and Singapore. Furthermore, it examines how these nations establish frameworks that adequately protect human embryos, given their unique moral status, while ensuring ethical standards within this research domain. Through this analysis, this book also seeks to contrast the regulatory approaches from the perspectives of developing and developed nations.

In conclusion, this chapter synthesises the findings of the entire book, demonstrating that although significant progress has been made in the ethical governance of stem cell research, ongoing discussions and potential reforms remain essential to addressing the inherent complexities and societal implications of advancements in this field. As technology evolves, so too must the frameworks that govern it, necessitating a dynamic regulatory environment. For instance, the recent ability to culture human embryos beyond 14 days following fertilisation raises critical questions regarding the need to extend

DOI: 10.4324/9781003583479-5

the statutory time limit. Adaptability is crucial in meeting new challenges and perspectives within a rapidly evolving research landscape while maintaining the primacy of human dignity and ethical integrity. The United Kingdom exemplifies this adaptability by consistently aligning its regulatory approach with scientific advancement, demonstrating a commitment to protecting the sanctity of human embryos alongside public interests—an approach from which Malaysia could learn.

5.2 Concluding insights on human stem cell research in Malaysia

Based on the examination of Malaysia's regulatory approach, particularly when compared to the practices of the United Kingdom and Singapore, this book concludes that Malaysia adopts a notably restrictive stance on the use of human embryos in stem cell research. This restrictive position stems from a cultural context, which is largely shaped by religious considerations as well as legal frameworks that prioritise caution over innovation. Within this context, Malaysia's regulatory environment lacks several key measures deemed essential for safeguarding human embryos and ensuring the promotion of ethical conduct and compliance in stem cell research activities. For instance, the absence of clear guidelines on the permissible use of human embryos in research and the lack of comprehensive licencing systems hinder the effectiveness of oversight.

Such shortcomings contribute to widespread concerns among local stakeholders, including researchers and ethicists who perceive the current regulatory environment as inadequate for preventing unethical practices. This perception not only jeopardises the credibility of the Malaysian stem cell research agenda but also risks alienating potential local and international collaborators who may be reluctant to engage with a framework that does not prioritise ethical standards that align with the regulatory practices of leading nations in this domain (Bin Abdul Aziz et al., 2018; Foong, 2012; Gopalan et al., 2020). This concern is particularly acute given the global advancements in stem cell research, which could overshadow Malaysia's contributions if the integrity of its practices cannot be assured.

As noted in the preceding chapter, these concerns are largely rooted in the existing governance framework which suffers from a lack of effective legal enforcement of their rules. This failure has resulted in a significant regulatory gap between the public and private sectors, suggesting that stem cell research in the private sector operates within a regulatory vacuum. This vacuum is characterised by the absence of legislation and consistent oversight mechanisms, which may lead to variability in compliance and oversight standards. Furthermore, the National Bioethics Council, which is intended to provide crucial ethical and policy guidance, has not played an active role in addressing these issues. This inactivity limits the potential for a cohesive regulatory approach, leaving researchers without the necessary support and guidance to conduct their work ethically and responsibly. If Malaysia does not implement necessary improvements to its governance framework, it risks hindering its ability to remain competitive in the rapidly evolving field of stem cell research. The following section highlights some potential measures for consideration to enhance Malaysia's regulatory landscape.

5.3 Summary of key findings

5.3.1 Revisiting the ban of embryo creation for stem cell research

The current prohibition on creating human embryos for research in Malaysia is largely shaped by the religious views of the National Fatwa Committee, which informs national guidelines. In contrast, the United Kingdom and Singapore incorporate a variety of expert opinions, including bioethics and religious perspectives. Malaysia should similarly engage a broader range of experts to foster a nuanced understanding of this prohibition and whether it is meaningfully justified. Moreover, it is crucial to require qualifications or justifications for the use of human embryos in research, ensuring that such use is genuinely necessary and cannot be achieved through alternative means.

This approach aligns with the concept of niyyah (intention) in Islamic ethics. One might question why the intentions behind using embryos for research have not been addressed in the current framework, particularly regarding the potential for allowing the creation of embryos. Such a justification could also resonate with other religious beliefs in the country. Furthermore, the notion of communal obligation may support the creation of human embryos when viable alternatives are lacking, especially if the research is deemed vital for humanity's benefit.

Additionally, it is essential for religious scholars in Malaysia to engage in cross-disciplinary and meaningful dialogue, as this may provide diverse perspectives and a better understanding of the scientific aspects involved. For example, as recorded in the UK Parliament Hansard, some Roman Catholic members of the House of Lords modified their views on embryo classification after observing a 4-day-old embryo under laboratory conditions.

5.3.2 The need for comprehensive discourse on the 14-day rule in Malaysia

Malaysia has adopted the 14-day rule for embryo development, similar to the United Kingdom and Singapore but treats it as a guideline rather than a legally enforceable limit, raising concerns about its effectiveness. There are calls to extend the rule to the creation of human embryos, arguing that legal status could enhance ethical considerations and protection for embryos.

While aligning with international standards is important, Malaysia should also explore the rule's relevance within its cultural and religious contexts, particularly Islamic beliefs about ensoulment at 120 days. Engaging in a discourse on potentially extending the rule based on scientific needs is essential, and the National Bioethics Council could lead this effort, providing a Malaysian perspective.

5.3.3 Ensuring consent provisions in research involving humans, embryos, and gametes

Consent is essential in research involving human participants. Although Malaysia mandates consent in its national guidelines, the application and enforcement of this requirement are questionable because it is not a statutory provision. Additionally, the national guidelines lack comprehensive criteria for obtaining consent, particularly when compared to the approaches of the United Kingdom and Singapore. To enhance the framework, the national guidelines should be revised to include more detailed requirements, and it would be beneficial for these requirements to hold legal weight, ensuring they apply to both public and private sectors.

5.3.4 Enhancing compliance through sanctioning strategy

While Malaysia appears to adopt a more restrictive regulatory approach compared to the United Kingdom and Singapore, an examination suggests that this may not effectively deter non-compliance due to the absence of sanctions for violations. The current rules, which are outlined only in national guidelines, prevent the Malaysian regulatory body from enforcing penalties for any infractions. In contrast, the United Kingdom and Singapore, despite their more permissive regulatory frameworks, implement stricter measures with better deterrence mechanisms. Their regulatory bodies have the authority to impose statutory penalties for the violation of laws governing the use of human embryos. To align with the regulatory practices of more experienced nations, Malaysia might consider introducing statutory penalties to enhance compliance.

5.3.5 Strengthening governance through a licencing and monitoring system

Currently, Malaysia does not have a licencing system governing the use of human embryos for research. Approval from the Institutional Review Board (IRB) or Independent Ethics Committee (IEC) is the only requirement outlined in the national guidelines. The National Stem Cell Research and Ethics Committee (NSCERT) has the authority to review any research at any time;

however, this lack of a standardised and consistent practice raises concerns about ethical compliance.

In contrast to the stringent licencing system implemented in the United Kingdom, the absence of a licencing framework in Malaysia hampers the regulatory body's ability to control the use of human embryos, potentially leading to unnecessary use and redundancy in research. A licencing system would necessitate a designated body to monitor and oversee compliance from the outset. Given the rapid advancements in human stem cell research (hSCR), an independent regulatory authority is crucial for maintaining a robust regulatory framework.

Moreover, the current system remains unclear as to how the government monitors the use of human embryos within the private sector or ensures compliance with the time limit. If ethical compliance is questionable even at the research stage, there are significant concerns about how authorities can guarantee that embryonic cells used in clinical research are sourced ethically. To avoid this regulatory gap, the licencing system will be an instrumental regulatory measure that needs to be adopted to further strengthen the governance framework in Malaysia.

If implementing a licencing system proves infeasible due to challenges such as limited resources and manpower, Malaysia could consider adopting a model similar to Singapore. In Singapore, the IRB conducts an initial review of applications, serving as the first tier of screening, followed by a requirement for approval from the Director of Health at the national level. This approach may provide a practical solution for Malaysia's regulatory needs.

5.3.6 Establishing legislation to protect human embryos in Malaysia

To enhance and strengthen Malaysia's regulatory framework, it is essential to implement a range of previously discussed measures alongside legally binding legislation. Malaysia's guidelines lack statutory authority and do not guarantee necessary legal protection for embryos rendering them more vulnerable than that of embryos used in jurisdictions with established laws. Establishing a comprehensive legal framework will address these regulatory gaps by creating enforceable standards for all types of research involving human embryos. This legally regulated environment would apply uniformly across both public and private sectors.

Implementing appropriate legislation would also empower Malaysian regulators at national and institutional levels. While statutory rules carry legal weight, they necessitate an enforcement body to ensure compliance and effective implementation. Moreover, legal rules can often be ambiguous; thus, establishing a dedicated regulatory authority is crucial for raising awareness and ensuring adherence to these regulations among all stakeholders.

However, considering Malaysia's status as a developing nation, the government may face funding challenges in creating a dedicated agency, similar to the UK's Human Fertilisation and Embryology Authority (HFEA), which could be prohibitively expensive. Alternatively, Malaysia could adopt a model similar to Singapore's approach, establishing legislation specifically for biomedical research that includes targeted regulations for this sensitive area. It is imperative for Malaysia to develop legislation governing research, as such legal frameworks are currently non-existent.

5.3.7 Bolstering the function of Malaysia's National Bioethics Council in addressing ethical challenges posed by emerging technologies

As Malaysia seeks to develop and advance stem cell research and other emerging technologies, it is vital to recognise the complex ethical dilemmas these innovations may present. Given that regulators and policymakers are often not well-equipped to navigate these intricate ethical issues, an advisory body composed of relevant experts plays a crucial role in providing policy guidance. This support can help policymakers make decisions regarding regulatory approaches that are acceptable to both local and international communities. To effectively establish and leverage ethical advisory bodies, Malaysia should take cues from other countries. While Malaysia has taken an initial step by forming its National Bioethics Council, there is a pressing need for this Council to adopt a more proactive role. The government must engage with the Council more actively. As demonstrated in the preceding chapter, advisory bodies in the United Kingdom and Singapore have significantly contributed to the development of regulations in their respective countries, a level of engagement that is currently lacking in Malaysia.

Furthermore, Malaysia must recognise the importance of capacity building in the field of ethics, which is still in its infancy within the country. For the ethics council to function effectively, it is essential to ensure that some of its members, if not all, possess the appropriate qualifications and a solid understanding of ethics. Additionally, this body should take a more active role in public education and awareness initiatives related to ethical issues.

5.4 Final reflections

The discussion revealed a lack of consensus on this controversial issue, both from philosophical and religious perspectives. However, it is noteworthy that all religious teachings addressed in this discussion emphasise the sanctity of life. While there is no unified viewpoint regarding whether human embryos prior to 14 days of development should be classified as human persons, there is a common understanding among these teachings that if the intention behind using human embryos is to generate greater benefits and alleviate human suffering, then such use is morally acceptable. Therefore, rather than continue debating when human life begins, the exact moment personhood emerges, or whether embryos less than 14 days old possess sentience—questions which may never have clear answers due to the polarised nature of the debate—the conversation should instead focus on the intentions behind using human embryos for research.

An examination of the governance frameworks in the United Kingdom, Singapore, and Malaysia reveals that Malaysia's current regulatory measures fall short of ensuring adequate protection for human embryos used in research and maintaining ethical compliance, despite its restrictive approach compared to other less-studied jurisdictions. Malaysia is in a unique position to learn from the experiences of established jurisdictions like the United Kingdom and Singapore in managing this contentious area of research, rather than attempting to reinvent the wheel. While the United Kingdom provides a comprehensive governance model, its implementation may be unfeasible for Malaysia as a developing nation with limited resources due to the legislative costs involved. Conversely, Singapore's framework may be more suitable, as it allows Malaysia to create a broad piece of legislation regulating all types of human biomedical research, complemented by specific regulations for restricted areas such as human embryonic research.

It is important to acknowledge that the options discussed in this book do not present a definitive solution. However, by outlining these options, the book paves the way for future scholarly work and offers policymakers a foundation to address the ethical issues associated with using human embryos, particularly in human stem cell research, and to better regulate this controversial field. To assess the practicality and applicability of these options within the Malaysian context, policymakers should engage in consultations with a variety of relevant stakeholders. In doing so, they can use the issues and findings reported as guideposts. The outcomes of these consultations can then be further analysed by experts, such as those from the National Bioethics Council.

Ultimately, it is hoped that this book will contribute to the literature and enhance understanding of the legal issues surrounding the use of human embryos in human stem cell research in Malaysia.

References

Bin Abdul Aziz, M. F., Morrison, M., & Kaye, J. (2018). Regulating human stem cell research and therapy in low-and middle-income countries: Malaysian perspectives. *New Genetics and Society*, *37*(1), 2–20.

Foong, P. (2012). The regulatory regime for human embryonic stem cell (HESC) research in Malaysia: A critique. *Jurnal Undang-undang dan Masyarakat*, *16*, 53.

Gopalan, N., Nor, S. N. M., & Mohamed, M. S. (2020). Regulation of stem cell technology in Malaysia: Current status and recommendations. *Science and Engineering Ethics*, *26*(1), 1–25. https://link.springer.com/article/10.1007/s11948-019-00111-5

House of Lords. (1989). Human Fertilisation and Embryology Bill. https://hansard.parliament.uk/Lords/1989-12-07/debates/124a72fc-9a83-477d-b3ad-8ae2b57c6520/HumanFertilisationAndEmbroyologyBillHl

Index

For Product Safety Concerns and Information please contact our EU
representative GPSR@taylorandfrancis.com
Taylor & Francis Verlag GmbH, Kaufingerstraße 24, 80331 München, Germany

www.ingramcontent.com/pod-product-compliance
Ingram Content Group UK Ltd.
Pitfield, Milton Keynes, MK11 3LW, UK
UKHW021245190926
475569UK00001BA/12
9781032951669